What Your Colleagues Are Saying

"Here is what I love about this book: It has gobs and gobs of student writing samples with smart and lively explanations of how to use each as the focus of a craft lesson to teach writing. The right models of student writing are the best mentor texts a teacher can find and with this book, you need look no further.... Breathe, fellow writing teachers. Much needed and wanted help has arrived."

—**RUTH CULHAM,** Author of *Traits Writing*

"Gretchen Bernabei is a wizard. In this book she provides wonderfully practical help for instruction in narrative, expository, and argumentative writing. And like all her work, it rests on a dynamic sense of 'structure.' At a time when writing instruction is becoming increasingly formulaic, Gretchen continues to show the wealth of options students can have for developing their ideas and expanding on their experiences."

—**THOMAS R. NEWKIRK,** Author of
Holding On to Good Ideas in a Time of Bad Ones

"Gretchen Bernabei has done it again—only better. *Fun-Size Academic Writing for Serious Learning* plops us down in the middle of the disheveled process of writing and gives us concrete ways to navigate through. This book stands apart in two ways. First, it gives us myriad unpublished mentor texts written by students with diverse abilities and backgrounds. Second, its a la carte format makes it a perfect resource from which teachers can cull lessons."

—**KAY SHURTLEFF,** Region 10 Education Service Center,
President, Texas Council of Teachers of English Language Arts

"Once again, Gretchen Bernabei weaves together masterful, concrete strategies with powerful student examples. Gretchen provides text structures and student models to move authentic writing beyond traditional formulas. This book is a must read/must try for all ELA teachers."

—**P. TIM MARTINDELL, EdD,**
President-Elect, Texas Council of Teachers of English Language Arts,
Past-President, West Houston Area Council of Teachers of English, and
Lecturer, Rice University Center for Continuing Studies, Teacher Certification

"The good news is that the book you hold in your hand is a lifeline to real writing instruction. Based on careful observation of wonderfully varied student writing, Grades 4–9, and organized around the genres of the Common Core Standards, *Fun-Size Academic Writing* is the best book I know for giving students a fun-size suit that fits their true voices as writers and thinkers."

—**BARRY LANE,** Founder of Discover Writing

Fun-Size Academic Writing
for Serious Learning

Dedicated to
students who love their writing,
and teachers who love their students.

—Gretchen Bernabei and Judi Reimer

Fun-Size Academic Writing
for Serious Learning

101 Lessons & Mentor Texts——Narrative, Opinion/Argument, & Informative/Explanatory, Grades 4—9

Gretchen Bernabei

Judi Reimer

Foreword by Barry Lane

CORWIN
LITERACY

CORWIN
A SAGE Company

FOR INFORMATION:

Corwin

A SAGE Company

2455 Teller Road

Thousand Oaks, California 91320

(800) 233-9936

www.corwin.com

SAGE Publications Ltd.

1 Oliver's Yard

55 City Road

London EC1Y 1SP

United Kingdom

SAGE Publications India Pvt. Ltd.

B 1/I 1 Mohan Cooperative Industrial Area

Mathura Road, New Delhi 110 044

India

SAGE Publications Asia-Pacific Pte. Ltd.

3 Church Street

#10-04 Samsung Hub

Singapore 049483

Publisher: Lisa Luedeke

Development Editor: Julie Nemer

Editorial Assistant: Francesca Dutra Africano

Production Editor: Melanie Birdsall

Copy Editor: Kim Husband

Typesetter: C&M Digitals (P) Ltd.

Proofreader: Ellen Brink

Cover Designer: Gail Buschman

Interior Designer: Anthony D. Paular

Copyright © 2013 by Corwin

Printed in the United States of America

Library of Congress Cataloging-in-Publication Data

Bernabei, Gretchen.

Fun-size academic writing for serious learning : 101 lessons & mentor texts—narrative, opinion/argument, & informative/explanatory, grades 4–9 / Gretchen Bernabei, Judi Reimer.

pages cm

ISBN 978-1-4522-6861-3 (pbk.)

1. English language—Composition and exercises—Study and teaching (Elementary)—Activity programs. 2. English language—Composition and exercises—Study and teaching (Middle school)—Activity programs. I. Reimer, Judi. II. Title.

LB1576.B4834 2013

372.6—dc23   2013018728

This book is printed on acid-free paper.

SUSTAINABLE FORESTRY INITIATIVE

Certified Chain of Custody
Promoting Sustainable Forestry
www.sfiprogram.org
SFI-01268

SFI label applies to text stock

13 14 15 16 17 10 9 8 7 6 5 4 3 2 1

Contents

Part II. Informative/Explanatory   90

Part III. Opinion/Argument 152

Appendixes

Visit the companion website at **www.corwin.com/funsize**
for downloadable versions of all the student
essays and text structures.

Foreword

A Tailor of Fun-Sized Suits

There is an old story about a wonderful tailor who makes the best suits. A man decides to go have a suit made by the tailor and he goes to his shop for a fitting. The man tries on the suit but the sleeve does not seem right.

He tells the tailor, "This sleeve does not fit."

The tailor eyes him up and down. Finally, he speaks. "I see the problem. It's your arm. You must hold it out straight in front of you."

Indeed, the man held out his arm in front of him, and the sleeve fell into place.

"You're right," the man said. "Thank you, but you know, this right pant leg seems a little long."

The tailor looked down. "I see the problem. "You must keep your right leg stiff and extend it behind you."

"You are so right," said the man. "It fits much better, but this other sleeve is now too long."

"No worries," said the tailor. "Just bend your elbow and suspend it in the air like this." The tailor bent the man's elbow.

"Perfect," said the man as he slowly limped out of the tailor's shop and into the street, dragging his stiff leg behind him, with his elbow crooked in the air and his other arm stretched out in front of him.

At this point, two little old ladies see the man coming out of the shop.

One turns to the other and says, "What a wonderful tailor! Look, the man is so crippled, yet the suit fits him so well!"

This story describes what's wrong with many traditional textbook program approaches to teaching nonfiction essay writing. Instead of liberating the unique voice of the writer, they conform the writer to a common monolithic template, such as the five-paragraph essay, the hamburger paragraph, the topic sentence and mandatory three supporting details, and so on and so on. If students succeed on a test using these ready-made formulas, everyone remarks, "What a wonderful program! The children are from such different economic backgrounds, yet they have all succeeded on the test." However, what they are really saying is, "The children are so unique, but have fitted their minds so successfully to this common boring template." Bravo!

In a flat world economy that depends on creativity and innovation, this is a tragedy of epic proportions for American education only exacerbated by a plethora of new, robot-scored, high-stakes writing tests, all of which claim close alignment with the Common Core State Standards. If we are not careful, writing will soon be seen as the act of formulating sentences and paragraphs to be scanned for syntactical structure and lexile level by machines. Yuck. All of this might be a bad science fiction movie if it weren't truly happening.

The good news is that the book you hold in your hand is a lifeline to real writing instruction. Based on careful observation of wonderfully varied student writing, Grades 4 through 12, and organized around the genres of the Common Core State Standards, *Fun-Size Academic Writing for Serious Learning* is the best book I know for giving students a fun-sized suit that fits their true voices as writers and thinkers. To the extent that all students seek deep engagement and joy in the task of nonfiction writing, we can say that all students come to class "fun-sized," and it is only bland, myopic curriculum that reduces their voices to uniform gray paragraphs that sound correct but say little.

The power of this immensely practical, kid-friendly book of craft lessons is that it teaches more than writing; rather, it teaches classical rhetoric, that ancient art of learning to say stuff different ways. For example, the Renaissance teacher Erasmus would be delighted to see that a fourth grader from Florida named Samantha has mastered his famous lesson, Scesis Onomoton, by writing about her blue-eyed Barbie doll, using different words to name the plastic figure each time she repeats it within a piece. The humor and voice in Samantha's writing makes it useful for teaching this valuable lesson at every grade level with joy and vigor. The same is true when an eighth grader named Eileen teaches us a lesson on literary analysis by writing about character tension, or when a tenth grader named Adrian teaches us a how to write powerful openings. Every writing teacher knows that the best lessons come directly from the classroom and student writing. These expert student authors will inspire those who use this book to discover this truth every day. After a few months of use, teachers will have their own inspiring examples to add to those Gretchen and Judi have collected.

Along with the dozens of simple two-page lessons, *Fun-Size Academic Writing for Serious Learning* provides a structural analysis of each piece of writing. Gretchen Bernabei introduced this dynamic concept of the kernel essay, back in 2003, in her groundbreaking book *Reviving the Essay: How to Teach Structure Without Formula*, and since then, teachers all around the country are learning to teach structure in a more playful and varied way that mirrors what real writers do at their desks. Experimenting with text structure like this is like extracting the DNA from a mentor text and showing all students how to reproduce something like it in a simple and direct way. For centuries, students in all fields have learned this way. The apprentice copies the work of the master and learns craft in the process. Since the masters in this book are students, there is extra motivation because students can see that the success of their peers is within their reach.

The other day I received an e-mail from a teacher friend who was trying to source a quote from me for a book she was writing. The quote was,

"I don't teach writing; I teach possibility."

If you are a language arts teacher and believe this quote, then you are very lucky indeed, because you are holding in your hand a writing lesson bible of rhetorical possibility to explore with your students for many years to come.

—Barry Lane

Acknowledgments

We are deeply grateful for the help of so many people: the Corwin Literacy twin titans, Lisa Luedeke and Maura Sullivan; our skillful Corwin team, including Julie Nemer, Francesca Dutra Africano, Melanie Birdsall, Kim Husband, Gail Buschman, and Jennifer Barron; for the brilliance of Thomas Newkirk; for the diligence of Alicia Narvaez; for the generosity of countless student writers and their passionate teachers, among whom are Pam Abbott, Angie Andrade, Brenda Armstrong, Melissa Bates, Courtney Bauer, Jeannine Bell, Macie Bemrick, Carol Bradshaw, Kathy Broussard, Abbey Bryan, Cynthia Candler, Kathleen Chupp, Gail Clark, Julie Corliss, Shelley Fisette, Neta Geeslin, Jody Giles, Heather Guerra, Jayne Hover, Tammy Joy, Larry Lacey, Jr., Joanna Minardi, Megan Pancone, Theresa Phelps, Denise Smith, Stacy Smith, Amy Stengel, Rebecca Tielking, Robin Whitehead, Mary Whitener, and Jenny Wilde.

We are indebted to the love and support of our families: Johnny, Julian and Matilde, and Dave.

—*Gretchen Bernabei and Judi Reimer*

Introduction

How This Book Began

One of the very first weird truths you learn about teaching is this: When kids hear something from other kids, they get it so much faster than when they hear the very same thing from us. It's inexplicable. But every teacher has seen it, no matter what the content.

You may be saying, "A concrete noun is something you can touch," and you see blinks.

One of them says, "Something you can touch?"

You say, "Yes, something you can touch." More blinks.

Then a kid pipes in. "Dude. You can touch it," and understanding dawns. Ohhh. You can *touch* it.

Maybe it doesn't matter how this happens, but just knowing that it does provides for us one of the very best tools in teaching. This book is built on two premises, and this is the first:

Students learn from each other faster and more deeply than they learn from us.

In *The Book of Learning and Forgetting*, Frank Smith (1998) opens our eyes about how the quickest, most powerful learning students do is by watching each other. We know this as parents, but we don't always remember it as teachers.

So one day, as we looked at student test essays that our state had released, we realized we'd discovered an instructional gold mine.

And the mining began.

We looked for and found high-scoring essays, obtained permissions from student writers and their parents, and began to explore ways to use these essays in our teaching, mostly as gallery walks.

But soon we realized how useful these essays could be for tightly focused, whole-group instruction in *craft*. Some demonstrated extraordinary word choice; some employed a sophisticated rhetorical device; some displayed an impressive range of sentence variety; some used powerful images. They were all enlightening in different ways. All provided opportunities to teach.

In fact, we discovered the gold mine extended beyond test essays. We began gathering all kinds of writing, at all different grade levels, from all over the country. The pieces we collected range from informal journal entries to formal literary analysis, but they all have one thing in common: There's a craft nugget in each.

Each craft nugget became the center of a lesson in this book. Using the student essay as a mentor text, we worked backward, designing a lesson based on each one that would teach students how to *recognize* and *replicate* the craft move in their own writing.

The results have been astounding. Teachers all over the country have tried out these lessons in workshops. Here is a sampling of their responses:

"I can't wait to get back to class and try these out!"

"My students will be able to do this!"

"I finally feel like I have a tangible plan for teaching writing, and not just guessing. I also think the kids will *enjoy* it!"

"As teachers, we should aim at starting small and building, and this provides the tools and structure to do this. It is workable and doable with any student!"

We've received hundreds of emails from teachers, and have been encouraged, too, by their students' responses:

"We used these lessons and our 50% benchmark scores jumped to 88% passing on The Test…"

"My students actually asked to keep writing, and I *never* thought I'd see that happen."

Success is transformative for everyone.

The Deception of "Show, Don't Tell"

Ironic, isn't it? Those "show, don't tell" posters we put up in our classrooms? They tell. And they don't show *how*.

It took us twenty-five years to notice the irony. Asking students to "show, don't tell," is telling. Without showing *how*. Showing *how* is difficult without student models. Each one of the unique pieces of student work in this book *shows how to show*, not tell.

When your students experience these fun-size lessons, when they see how to show, you'll hear, "I can do that." When they hear the voices of other students, you'll see the understanding dawning. It's so palpable, you can touch it. Dude.

How the Lessons Work

We've divided up the book into the main kinds of writing taught, tested, and even outlined in the Common Core State Standards:

- narrative

- opinion/argument

- informative/explanatory

The sample pieces we have gathered fall into these main categories. Some states may use different language. For example, what Texas assesses as "expository" at Grades 4, 7, and 9 is known to the rest of the world as "argument." Persuasive writing, likewise, falls under the category of "argument" for the purposes of this book. Any teacher who is looking for a "how-to" or procedural paper will find it in the "informative/explanatory" section.

Each craft lesson is divided into sections:

- **What Writers Do:** describes a craft move that writers might make

- **What This Writer Does:** pinpoints that move in this specific piece

- **Activity for Your Class:** asks students to reread, identify something, and manipulate it in the student sample

- **Challenge for Students:** invites students to try out this move in their own writing

At the bottom of each craft lesson, we've also included the *text structure* of the piece. This isn't part of the craft lesson but an added feature. One way teachers ask their students to develop essays is to begin with a structure. We place one sentence in each box in the structure to create what we call a "kernel essay" that's modeled on the student mentor text used in that craft lesson. A "kernel essay" is like a kernel of corn, tiny but packed (Bernabei, Hover, & Candler, 2009). The structure, when imitated, provides students with a kernel of an essay.

A collection of text structures like these can help students make organizational choices. You will find the collection of structures at the back of this book. (For more on this feature of the lessons, see How to Use Text Structures on page 6.)

Should the lessons be done in order? No. You should pick and choose on your own and will undoubtedly develop your own favorites.

Soon, you'll have student writing from your own class to demonstrate the craft lessons here, but these pieces of writing are a great starter set. We suggest that as your students write, you might keep some of their writing to use with the craft lessons, replacing the student pieces here. Your students will react more strongly when they recognize the names of the writers. But they will have no trouble identifying real student voices, even when the students come from another school.

You can use any lesson to jump-start and guide students as they begin a new piece of writing or to help them revise and enrich pieces they already have under way.

How to Find Quick Solutions to Writing Problems

What causes students to fail writing assignments or writing tests? Basically the same short list of problems:

- writing that wanders around without a plan

- vague writing

- not enough writing

- listy writing

- disconnected writing

- wordy writing

- boring writing

The lessons in this book focus on *solutions* to these problems. As you browse the table of contents, you will see that the craft lessons explicitly teach solutions, with those solutions modeled in the student pieces.

Learning to Read as Writers

At a recent NCTE conference, Kelly Gallagher talked about the importance of showing students mentor texts, texts written by professionals as well as student models. He said that he uses only excellent writing as mentor texts because "students see enough bad writing." We see his point.

But in *Teaching the Universe of Discourse*, James Moffett (1986) wondered at the wisdom of expecting students to imitate the prose of John Steinbeck. And Frank Smith's point that students learn most easily from watching the moves of other students is undeniable, too. To us, it is essential for students to see writing in all its various stages, the moves writers make along the way: in early forms, in developed forms, in polished forms.

How will they learn the habits of choice without seeing those choices in action? This leads to the second premise of our book:

Writers make choices.

Classrooms that show extraordinary student gains are classrooms with a safe writing climate. We create safe writing climates in our classrooms only by treating pieces of writing with respect. Most pieces of writing aren't finished, rubric-ready, evaluatable corpses. They are living, growing, organic, in-progress, complex groups of choices. The writer's question should not be, "*Is it done yet?*" or "*What grade did I get?*" but...

- "*What next?*"

- "*How does this work when you read it?*"

- "*What if we tinker with this or that... ?*"

This is how real writers work.

The pieces we share in class are conversations—breathing, ongoing, and revisable. Instead of "grading" a piece when they read it, it's much healthier and much more conducive to learning for students to read like a writer: to see, name, and learn from the moves the writer makes. Our goal is for students to

- accumulate choices

- enjoy the freedom to try out those choices

- get feedback from readers about how well their choices worked

This process is at the heart of learning to be an effective writer.

Or, to look at it another way, students might read a piece of writing—early, developed, polished, or Shakespearean—with this curiosity, through this lens:

- *What choices has this writer made?*

- *What structural moves?*

- *What detailing moves?*
- *What polishing moves?*
- *...and how do those moves work out?*

As students learn these moves from each other, they gain independence from us.

Naturally, we left some mistakes in. Some of these pieces were actually written in timed settings on "test day" of the state writing test. Some were written as classroom benchmark tests, some as regular classroom pieces. Some classroom pieces, of course, are more polished than others, having benefited from spell-check, conferencing with teachers or peers, proofreading steps, reference materials, and time. **It does some students a world of good to see mistakes in a high-quality piece**, potentially calming that demon-teacher-voice in their heads that shrieks at them, "If you can't write it perfectly, don't write it at all!"

If you wonder why we didn't clean them up, why we're modeling incorrectness, that's why. These are not corrected for perfection. There's not a paper written anywhere that couldn't stand a little more reworking or more editing. But each of these pieces does something magnificent, and we think it's good modeling to focus on *that*. We believe the most productive thing we can do is to notice strengths and build on them.

About the Grade Levels

At the top of each lesson, we included the grade level of the writer. We did this simply because it's interesting. But does that mean when I teach my fifth-grade class, I shouldn't use fourth-grade pieces? Or tenth? Of course not.

We learned long ago from Kenneth Koch's *Rose, Where Did You Get That Red?* (1973) that second graders can look at and imitate the masters. The opposite is also true. Older students can focus on and imitate moves made by younger writers as well. We remember well watching tenth graders absorb a lesson delivered via a fourth grader's writing. The tenth graders learned how to look for, find, and then plant different kinds of text in their writing, and the lesson stuck. Of course, the content of older writers' works will be different from the content used by younger students, but craft is for everyone. Anyone can use any lesson with any level. The teacher is the best judge of timing.

Again, classrooms that show extraordinary student gains are those that create a safe writing climate. We create safe writing climates in our classrooms one way: by treating pieces of writing with respect.

How to Use Text Structures

What are these boxes on the bottoms of the pages and what can you do with them?

As we mentioned above, those boxes are a graphic representation of the text structure used by the writer. Each structure provides us with dynamic additional activities for these lessons.

Guided by the structure, which is the "blueprint" of the piece, students can collaboratively deconstruct an essay and strip it down to its kernel essay form. A kernel essay consists of one sentence for each part of the structure.

To collaboratively analyze the essay, take the following steps:

1. Give each student a copy of the student essay.

2. Read the piece of writing.

3. Show the text structure to the students.

4. Ask students to circle the parts of the essay that match each box in the text structure.

5. Ask students to write a one-sentence summary for each circled chunk of text.

6. Take turns reading the summary sentences aloud to hear the kernel essay of the piece.

To use the structure to generate new writing, continue with these steps:

1. Look again at the structure.

2. Invite students to write their own content for the structure, writing one sentence for each box of the text.

3. Flesh out the sentences with details to create a full essay.

Here is an illustration of the steps outlined above:

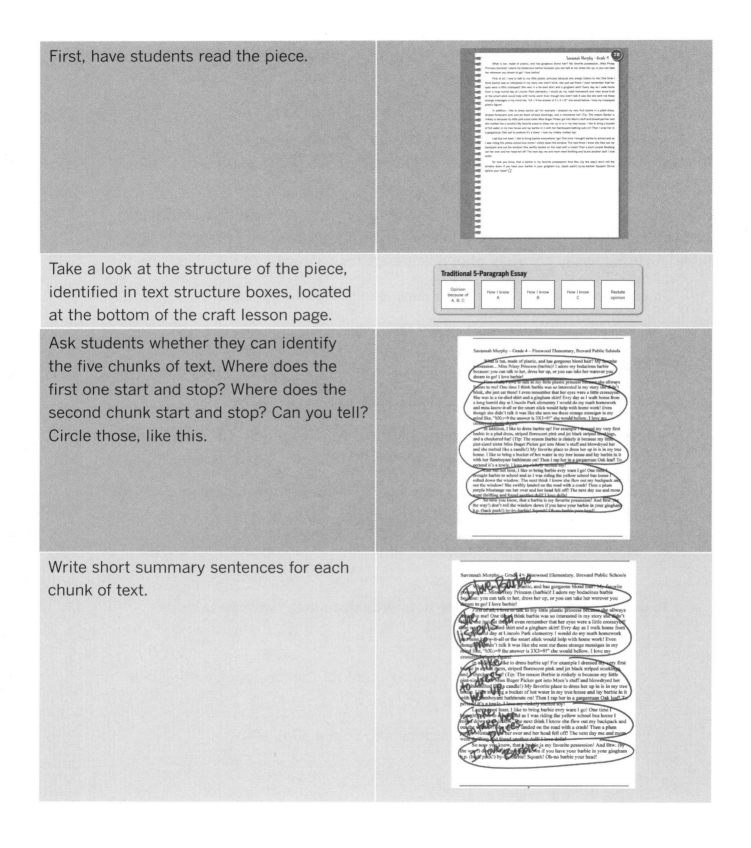

First, have students read the piece.

Take a look at the structure of the piece, identified in text structure boxes, located at the bottom of the craft lesson page.

Ask students whether they can identify the five chunks of text. Where does the first one start and stop? Where does the second chunk start and stop? Can you tell? Circle those, like this.

Write short summary sentences for each chunk of text.

Read the short sentences aloud to hear the kernel essay. (A kernel essay is one sentence for each part of the structure.)	*I love Barbie.* *She listens to me.* *I like to dress her up.* *I like to take her places.* *I love Barbie.*
Look again at the text structure.	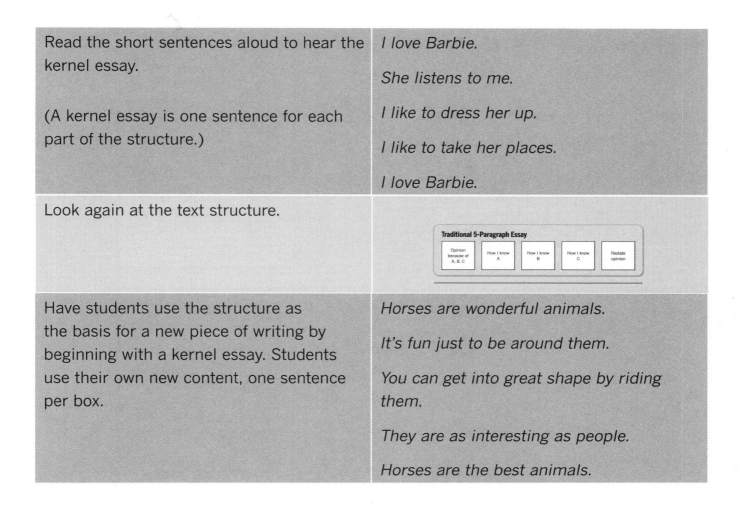
Have students use the structure as the basis for a new piece of writing by beginning with a kernel essay. Students use their own new content, one sentence per box.	*Horses are wonderful animals.* *It's fun just to be around them.* *You can get into great shape by riding them.* *They are as interesting as people.* *Horses are the best animals.*

Here is how the process would look on another piece, a narrative, with a different text structure.

First, have students read the piece.	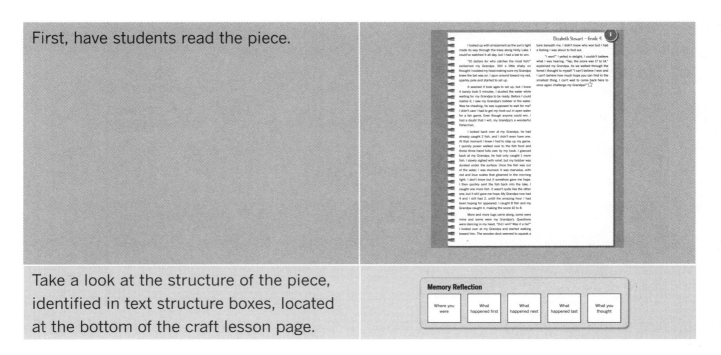
Take a look at the structure of the piece, identified in text structure boxes, located at the bottom of the craft lesson page.	

Ask students whether they can identify the five chunks of text. Where does the first one start and stop? Where does the second chunk start and stop? Can you tell? Circle those, like this.	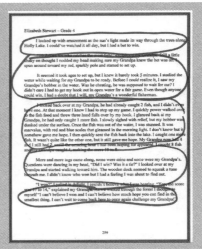
Write short summary sentences for each chunk of text.	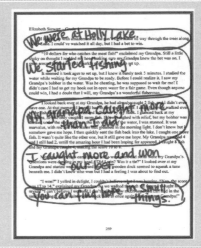
Read the short sentences aloud to hear the kernel essay. (A kernel essay is one sentence for each part of the structure.)	*We were at Holly Lake.* *We started fishing.* *My grandpa caught more than I did.* *I caught more and won our bet.* *You can find hope in small things.*
Look again at the text structure.	
Use the structure for a new piece by writing a kernel essay with new content, one sentence per box.	*Julian was in the living room.* *He bit down on his pizza slice and started to cry.* *His tooth almost came out.* *It finally came out after he went to bed.* *Nobody can be happy when their children are afraid.*

We included the text structure for every piece of writing to widen your instructional choices.

You may notice in the first example and in some other places in the book a text structure labeled "Traditional 5-Paragraph Essay." I am not a fan of teaching students this structure exclusively, as I hope the lessons throughout this book demonstrate! But I do think it's important that students learn to jump through any situational hoop that their academic life hands them. And some teachers in their futures will insist on this particular structure. Beyond that, though, for the function of this book, it's important to me that you see that this structure, *along with many others*, can work for a variety of purposes.

As a class, if you build a collection of text structures that you find useful, students may find themselves harvesting text structures from surprising sources and filling them with their own content—with surprising results.

Whether you begin with the text structures or the craft lessons that go with each piece of writing, we hope that you will enjoy the play of learning with the models and revel in the writing that your students produce.

Have a great time with these!

References

Bernabei, G. S., Hover, J., & Candler, C. (2009). *Crunchtime: Lessons to help students blow the roof off writing tests—and become better writers in the process*. Portsmouth, NH: Heinemann.

Koch, K. (1973). *Rose, where did you get that red?* New York: Random House.

Moffett, J. (1986). *Teaching the universe of discourse*. Boston: Houghton Mifflin.

Smith, F. (1998). *The book of learning and forgetting*. New York: Teachers College.

PART I

A Note About Narrative Writing

Narratives are stories, whether fiction or nonfiction. This broad category includes personal narratives, memoir, historical narratives, historical fiction, fantasy fiction, short stories, myths, parables, and narrative nonfiction of the kind found in many magazines.

Narratives can be used for many purposes. They can be used to make an argument (parables, fables, cautionary tales); they can be used for explaining information (biography, scientific processes, current events). Storytelling in the real world can be a way to present an argument or present information.

However, in our current reality, narratives are often treated as a separate genre in high-stakes testing situations. For this reason, we decided to create a separate section on narratives. We hope this eases some pressure on teachers who must prepare students for such a test. We would like to note, however, that trying to isolate narrative from argument and information is about as silly as separating creative writing from academic writing.

In our opening lesson, student writer Elizabeth Stewart offers a splendid memory of her grandfather. Her piece models both the structure of a narrative and a wonderful starter set of *types of details.* If you only use one craft lesson from the whole book, let it be this one.

Color It Up

> **What Writers Do** — Writers describe what they see, think, do, and say to tell a story. They describe what other characters do and say, too.
>
> **What This Writer Does** — Elizabeth skillfully blends all four kinds of description in this piece, leaving readers with a perfectly clear picture of the whole memory.

Activity for your class:

1. Pass out copies and read the piece together with your class.

2. Have students highlight the following:
   - yellow—everything the narrator thought
   - blue—everything the narrator saw
   - pink—everything that anyone said
   - green—everything anyone did (not counting thinking or talking)

(This highlighting can be done by groups, partners, or individuals.)

3. Share and compare what you notice.

4. Create a class chart so that your class can remember the colors.

Challenge for students:

Highlight a story you've written, using the same color codes, just to see your own patterns. You may want to use the Memory Reflection text structure, below, to write a new personal narrative.

Memory Reflection

Where you were	What happened first	What happened next	What happened last	What you thought

I looked up with amazement as the sun's light made its way through the trees along Holly Lake. I could've watched it all day, but I had a bet to win.

"10 dollars for who catches the most fish!" exclaimed my Grandpa. Still a little shaky on thought I nodded my head making sure my Grandpa knew the bet was on. I spun around toward my red, sparkly pole and started to set up.

It seemed it took ages to set up, but I knew it barely took 5 minutes. I studied the water while waiting for my Grandpa to be ready. Before I could realize it, I saw my Grandpa's bobber in the water. Was he cheating, he was supposed to wait for me? I didn't care I had to get my hook out in open water for a fair game. Even though anyone could win, I had a doubt that I will, my Grandpa's a wonderful fisherman.

I looked back over at my Grandpa, he had already caught 2 fish, and I didn't even have one. At that moment I knew I had to step up my game. I quickly power walked over to the fish food and threw three hand fulls over by my hook. I glanced back at my Grandpa, he had only caught 1 more fish. I slowly sighed with relief, but my bobber was dunked under the surface. Once the fish was out of the water, I was stunned. It was marvalus, with red and blue scales that gleamed in the morning light. I don't know but it somehow gave me hope. I then quickly sent the fish back into the lake. I caught one more fish. It wasn't quite like the other one, but it still gave me hope. My Grandpa now had 4 and I still had 2, untill the amazing hour I had been hoping for appeared. I caught 8 fish and my Grandpa caught 4, making the score 10 to 8.

More and more tugs came along, some were mine and some were my Grandpa's. Questions were dancing in my head, "Did I win? Was it a tie?" I looked over at my Grandpa and started walking toward him. The wooden dock seemed to squeak a tune beneath me. I didn't know who won but I had a feeling I was about to find out.

"I won?" I yelled in delight, I couldn't believe what I was hearing. "Yep, the score was 17 to 14," explained my Grandpa. As we walked through the forest I thought to myself "I can't believe I won and I can't believe how much hope you can find in the smallest thing. I can't wait to come back here to once again challenge my Grandpa!" ☆

Sprinkling Writing With Humor

What Writers Do — Writers sometimes make their readers laugh out loud. Adding humor is one way to keep readers reading.

What This Writer Does — In her personal narrative about "a time you helped someone," Aine makes readers to laugh out loud and beg, "Again!"

Activity for your class:

1. Read the piece aloud or choose a student volunteer who will read with lots of animation.

2. After passing out copies, have students reread it, highlighting their three favorite lines.

3. Compare favorites and talk about why students chose the lines they did.

4. Notice how many readers chose lines because they were funny.

Challenge for students:

Write a composition about a memory, and see if you can sprinkle some humor into it. See if you can make your readers laugh. You can use the text structure below if you wish.

Memory Reflection

Where you were	What happened first	What happened next	What happened last	What you thought

Have you ever helped someone because he was your best friend? Well I have…and I never will again.

My friend Mark took me by the hand and dragged me to the school's wall. He popped his bright pink bubble gum bubble in my face. "Listen" he said. "I have a football game in Denver tomorrow, and I can't miss it."

"Okay" I said, "What about it?"

"Can you watch Rex?" he asked. Now I've watched his ant farm, his pet taranchula, and even his mouse. But Rex…NO WAY! I was not going to watch the dog who ripped my pants, ate my 50,000 dollar retainer, and bites me every week. "Come on," he said. "I'll take you to the Beatles concert."

"Okay" I said, being a little hesitant.

"Tomorrow morning at 8:00."

"Got it," I said.

When I got to his house the next morning, I saw Rex through the fence with his teeth oozing with spit.

"Hey," Mark yelled, "Come on in!" I ran inside and sat on a brown leather chair. "Here's his dog food, he said handing me a big blue bag. "He needs to be fed twice a day and you can let him out three times every day."

"Anything else?" I asked.

"Nope, just don't take him off his chain." Mark ran out the door, and drove off with his parents. I walked home and thought "this won't be so bad after all."

The next morning my mom drove me to Mark's house on her way to the grocery store. I got out of the car and ran inside the house. I picked up his food bowl and went to the back door. I opened it just a crack and peeked outside and there was Rex laying on the grass looking like he was going to cry. I walked over to him and put the food bowl on the ground. I unhooked the chain and…it was the worst mistake of my life. Rex darted toward me and ripped my pants, again! I was furious, but so was he. I ran to the fence and started to climb it. Jumped over it and my shoe fell off. I watched as he ripped the laces to shreds.

I ran home screaming like a girl. I bought Rex a shock collar and I am never going to feed him again. So now Mark asks Jimmy, a strong kid to feed him. I'll stick with my bunnies even though I love dogs. That day was truly the worst time I helped someone. ☆

Adding Movement and Sound to Animate a Piece

What Writers Do — Writers sometimes liven up a piece of writing by adding movement and sound. This gives the action a boost and helps keep readers interested.

What This Writer Does — Alyssa retells a family memory, animating her scene with swifter-than-life motion and louder-than-life volume.

Activity for your class:

1. Distribute copies and have students read the piece.

2. Invite them to read it again, highlighting the following:

   - green—any words and phrases that show fast or intense movement
   - pink—any words and phrases that show loud voices or noises

3. Discuss what would happen if you replaced the highlighted words with drab words like *went* or *said*. Notice how the piece loses some of its animation or color.

Challenge for students:

Write about one moment in your day. Trade papers with a partner. Replace the drab verbs with animated verbs, like Alyssa used, and listen to the cartoon-like tone of the revised piece.

OR

Write about one moment in your day. Then find places to use phrases like Alyssa's to liven up your piece.

Memory Reflection

Where you were	What happened first	What happened next	What happened last	What you thought

Monkey Pajamas

"I want my monkey pajamas!" screamed my little sister Carolyn with a mad look on her face. "Be quiet, I've told you one million times we don't know where they are," exclaimed my big sister Mercedes. "Stop it you two or else I'll make both of you stick a sock full of rocks into your mouths," I yelled to them at the top of my lungs. "I want my pajamas!" Carolyn yelled again.

"I've got it," I said. Let's have a scavenger hunt. "Yea!" said Carolyn. "Fine" said Mercedes with a very glum look on her face.

I explained the rules and we began. Mercedes and I looked for about five minutes, then we got tired because it was 9:00 p.m. and we had school the next day. We turned on the news in my mom's room for my mom then we went to our rooms, not knowing that Carolyn was missing.

So I turned on the TV and put it on the show "Toddlers and Tiaras." All of a sudden Mercedes rushed into my room.

"Carolyn's missing! Help me look for her!" she screamed, with a worried look on her face. "Okay, Alyssa the great to the rescue." "No time for foolishness," said Mercedes as she was shoving me out of my room. "Carolyn's missing" we both yelled to my mom, as we quickly rushed to her room. "What?" yelled my mom in shock. "Well we need to look for her," she said. Okay said Mercedes and "Carolyn," we all shouted. "Where are you?" We split up in different directions. I went to my room, Mercedes went to hers, and my mom went to her room. I looked all over my room. I could not find her. I looked in my closet, under the covers of my bed, and looked in my bathroom. The only thing I found under my bed was one pair of shoes. My heart was pounding, I was thinking what happend, and I was getting really scared.

Then I heard a giggle and I heard it from under the bed. I looked under the bed and I saw a face. It was Carolyn! I was so happy and I gave her a big hug and she went to sleep in her penguin pajamas. ☆

Using Asides

> **What Writers Do** — Writers sometimes use asides to provide additional information (but usually just to whisper private secrets to the reader).
>
> **What This Writer Does** — Angelica uses several chatty and effective asides, punctuating them with parentheses, which add voice and depth to this piece.

Activity for your class:

1. Pass out copies and read the piece with students.

2. Ask them to highlight the words and phrases in parentheses, explaining that these are called "asides."

3. Next, have partners look together at the sentences in the asides. Then have them read the piece together. The first partner will read the main piece while the second will read the asides within the parentheses.

4. As a class, talk about what you notice.

Challenge for students:

Try adding several asides to your next piece of writing. You can write them while you're drafting the piece or add them in as a revision step.

Memory Reflection

Where you were	What happened first	What happened next	What happened last	What you thought

Have you ever helped someone? Don't lie to me, I know you have! Everyone has at some point in their life. Even you! And I have too. No kidding! More than once actually. Many times.

One of those many times was the one when I helped a bird. I found him/her in my back yard. A waterfall of tears cascaded from my eyes as it became clearer and clearer to me that this poor little fellow was dead. Every minute the bones seemed to creep further out of the little bird's lifeless body. The ants would jerk the skin and the flesh would slide off of bone like a curtain sliding off of the beginning of some gruesome, bloody play.

Soon, the sight was so unbearable that I could not stand it any longer. I rushed inside, nearly ripping the door off its hinges in the hurry, and got a box. It was small, square, and the perfect size for my little friend. I carefully cut a piece of green foam about the size of my box, and set it there. I then put the lid of the box on top. Standing tiptoe on a chair (it was one of the chairs that spins, and was making me very nervous as I swirled about atop it) I finally managed to grab (well, more knock down) a huge box of cloth from the top of my mom's dresser. From it, I selected a piece of purple satin, and a piece of purple silk. These I carefully glued on top of my box. Then I grabbed it, and ran back outside, forgetting the mess in my rush. Then, I took one look at the bird, thought about having to touch it, and ran back inside to get my mom.

When we were all back outside again, my mom gently picked up the bird and put him/her (I'm still not really sure...) into his/her casket. We then got out our shovels and dug a deep, deep hole. We carefully carried our little friend over to the hole, and bent down to place him in it. A single tear fell onto the little box before it was buried forever. A shell was set where he was buried, to remember him by. It is still there today.

I feel like I did the right thing, putting him to rest. There's a real truism in that. A truism is a catchy little saying that tells the moral or life lesson of the story. Something like don't judge a book by its cover. Everything has a truism, and this story's truism is that you can always help someone even if they're not human! ☆

Combining Rhetorical Devices: Cataloguing and Repetition

What Writers Do — Writers sometimes use combinations of rhetorical devices to increase reader interest.

What This Writer Does — Ashlea combines *cataloguing* (listing) and *repetition* (repeated words, phrases, or sentences) in her spectacular narrative about a camping trip.

Activity for your class:

1. Read the piece with students after passing out copies.

2. Ask them to look at the sentence in the first paragraph beginning "I couldn't roast…"

3. Next, ask a student to read that sentence aloud. As it's read, have the class listen for the list (*gooey, chewy marshmallows, go fishing in the bay, hike to the top of the fifteenth highest mountain in the U.S.A., or rock climb up "Ten Teeth Peak"*). Demonstrate by holding up fingers as it is read to count the items on the list.

4. Explain to students that the name for this device is *cataloguing:* making a good, long list of specific items.

5. Then ask students to find where the catalogued sentence is repeated toward the end. What is the effect of this repetition? (*It almost creates an inside joke between the reader and the writer.*)

Challenge for students:

Look through your journal or writer's notebook for a phrase like "lots of things" or "different kinds of…" Try replacing the phrase with a sentence using cataloguing and see what you think of the results. Experiment with repeating it.

Memory Reflection

Where you were	What happened first	What happened next	What happened last	What you thought

Cruel Camping in Colorado

The lightning flashed, the thunder roared and a big fat drop of mucky water landed in my newly highlighted hair. "Gaa." I mumbled. This was not a good start to my tenth birthday. My dad even promised me this would be my "Birthday spectacular." Birthday spectacular? How about birthday stinker! I couldn't roast gooey, chewy marshmellows, go fishing in the bay, hike to the top of the fifteenth highest mountain in the U.S.A., or rock climb up "Ten Teeth Peak." Instead of all that great, fun stuff, I was cramped in a leaking tent with my hopeful parents. My brother even got to sleep in his own tent. Then, all of the sudden there was a snuffling of leaves in the distance. Since I had been camping many times before, I knew that was not the typical forest floor creature. "Dad! Dad! Wake up!" my dad woke with a congested snore. "Aghh! Can't you remember to use that mouthwash I brought for you? Wo-we!" I snorted. My dad ignoring that replied, "You're fine Big girl. Go on back to bed." Once again, the lightning flashed while the thunder roared on. I pressed my face against the bug-pruff window to get some fresh air and a view, but what I got was some lousy brownish-greenish sky, and a smell of mud and dead bugs. That was definitely cruel camping in Colorado.

There it was again! That-that shuffling noise! It was coming closer, closer, closer, and closer... "Aghhh!" I screeched as loud as my voice box would go. "What was that?" My mom had woke. "Owwwwww!" my dad groaned annoyed. "You just hit my head!" he added. "Well, you hit my arm and you've been snoring all night long!" my mom grunted between her teeth. I chuckled to myself, listening to their childish argument. After a moment or two I told them what I had heard. "Stomping, and crashing, and tearing down anything and everything in its way. Clawing down trees and probably jumping over Ten Teeth Peak this very moment. It's got to be Ten Teeth's legendary 350 pound bear!" I explained, exsagerating just a tad. "That sounds like some old campfire story," assured my dad. "Besides, that bear is just some myth," my mom added. "You're right," I replied. Though I had no idea what was in store for me in just five minutes...

"But, I guess if you're so unsure of this, I bet we could go check out whatever's out there," my mother exclaimed suspiciously. "Ooookay?" I replied hesitantly. Once we got on our boots, we headed out. "This is kind of freaky!" I whispered softly to myself. The owls hooting, green mysterious eyes watching our every move, kind of gave me the willies. "Da-na, da-na, na-na, na-na!" went a little voice in my head just like in the movie, "Jaws." The next thing I knew, my mom yelped, "BEAR!" (BEAR!) "Ahhhhg!" I blurted as I jumped in the air, screaming for dear life, but knowing I would never make it out of here alive. Just as I made two full 360 degree turns without touching the ground, I landed in a ginormus puddle of goop and mud. I rolled over with mud slathered on my body, head to toe to say goodbye to my beloved parents one last time before my life ended... But they were laughing uncontrollably "Whaa?" I questioned. I looked to my right and noticed that my brother, Luke, who was supposed to be sleeping in his tent, was dressed in a bear costume! "Happy birthday!" they all laughed. I threw gooey mud at all of them. "That's what you get!" I taunted, laughing a little myself. "That wasn't very nice!" I complained. "Well, I guess we wanted to give you an extra special birthday present this year," Luke grined. I smiled back.

Well, the day after the incident, the bad weather had cleared out, so it dried up all the rain. Then I did roast gooey, chewy marshmellows, go fishing in the bay, hike to the top of the fifteenth highest mountain in the U.S.A., and rock climbed up to the tipy-top of "Ten Teeth Peak."

Some people say they found a puppy and got to keep it. Others say they found a doll they've been searching for, then finally found it. Though my story is about how I found a closer relationship with my family. I think that's the best thing you could ever find. I'm very proud of my parents and Luke for always trying to make our holidays and vacations fun. I am very blessed to have a family that cares so much about me. Luke better watch out though, because he's having a sleep-over this Friday night, and I might just borrow my friend Megan's clown wig. Mom had joked once about his fear of clowns. His sleep-over might just turn into a 3 ring circus... ☆

Using Literary Characters to Write Fiction

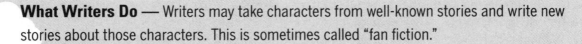

What Writers Do — Writers may take characters from well-known stories and write new stories about those characters. This is sometimes called "fan fiction."

What This Writer Does — Cherilyn crafts a new episode for *The Wizard of Oz*, borrowing Dorothy and the Wicked Witch. She uses this episode to prove her central thought or truism.

Activity for your class:

1. Read the piece together after giving students copies.

2. Have small groups find and highlight the following parts of the story:
   - yellow—the most important words and phrases that were taken directly from *The Wizard of Oz*
   - blue—the most important words or phrases that Cherilyn invented
   - green—the moral of the story

Challenge for students:

Choose a moral or truism of your own. Then try borrowing characters from a well-known story to put in an episode that proves your truism.

OR

Write a new episode first and see what moral or truism develops. You could use the text structure below to help you.

A Completely Made-Up Story

Characters doing something	Problem arises	How they try to solve it	How they do solve it

---

Do you know the story of The *Wizard of Oz*, when Dorothy meets strange creatures, and they help her get things for the Witch and then return home? Well, that was just part one. The story that I'm about to tell you is the other half that tells you the whole thing.

It was a rainy Saturday morning, when I was cheerfully eating my Cinnamon Toast Crunch, reading *The Wizard of Oz* book. Suddenly, like a snap of a finger, my glistening silver spoon anxiously came to life. It grumpily cried out, "Hurry up and make a wish in five, four, three," I had to think quick. The words "Go inside the book with Dorothy!" just rolled out of my tongue. All of a sudden a blue light mist surrounded me, and it forced me up the breakfast table, and into the maroon colored book. It felt like I was being pulled into a magnet. With such effort, it seemed my body was about to shatter into a million pieces. My feet soon had a surprisingly great shock wave, as it safely landed on a green pasture that was looking over a village called Honey Wheat Villa.

The confusing scene was such a blur, I didn't even realize that Dorothy in a blue calico dress was crying a river of tears onto the rich soil. Her cheeks were flustered with redness, while her eyes were flooded with salty liquid. After she had calmed down, I questioned the girl what was the matter. She slowly replied, "I succeeded on making my way towards home, but because I was hungry, I went to my favorite bakery shop— Billy's Baking Delight. But when I entered, the whole place was in ruins! And there was the evil Witch standing in the middle of the shop, wearing a wicked grin!" I thought to myself, I wonder if the Witch had already known that Dorothy would visit the bakery, or was just a lucky guess?" I dumbfoundedly stared at the sobbing girl, until suddenly, I came up with a brilliant plan to get rid of the devastating Witch.

In my mind, I came up with a tremendous solution that'll make Dorothy explode out into space with happiness. Since the Witch hates sweet foods, such as frosting, we could get ten cans of that substance and squirt it all over the Witch's body. She will soon melt, while Dorothy and I will put her liquid-self into a jar. Then we'll throw it in the deep, blue sea to be lost forever. I told that to my new friend, and she instantly stopped her nonsense, a sly grin slowly starting on her shining face. The next day at dawn, the two of us went to the grocery shop and met at Billy's Baking Delight. We did just like what I had wanted it to go. After exactly fifty-nine minutes and fifty-nine seconds, it was a calamity in the room. But the peculiar thing is, smack dab in the middle, lay a still, black puddle of a melted, now gone Witch.

The point of the adventure that I had was to show you that helping someone doesn't always have to be evil, but it can also earn you friend. ☆

Using Specific Language From a Special Setting

What Writers Do — Writers can thrust the reader into a different world by using specialized vocabulary from that world.

What This Writer Does — In his fantasy story about playing in the Super Bowl, David uses specific terminology from the world of football (height, weight, names, plays) to paint for readers what it would be like to be suddenly thrust into a dramatic moment.

Activity for your class:

1. Pass out copies of the story.

2. Read the story aloud as students follow along on their copies.

3. Have students circle the text from *"Where are we?"* to *"scored the game-winning touchdown in the Super Bowl"* in the next-to-last sentence.

4. Ask them to highlight any words or phrases within the circled text that:
    *   are from the football world
    *   help to describe the setting

5. Discuss with the class the importance of using language to capture a sense of place and a particular dramatic moment.

Challenge for students:

Pick a dramatic moment from sports, history, a book, or a movie. Using the text structure below, write about stepping into that world during a dramatic moment. See how much language from that world you can include.

Plunging Into a Different World

What I was doing	What caused the magic transport	Where I found myself	What happened next	What I think now, looking back

"What do you want to do?!" my best friend, Kyle, asked me. "I don't know," I moaned. We had been sitting on the couch staring at a blank T.V. ever since the power went out an hour ago. We were bored to death. "Wanna get a snack?" I suggested. "Sure," Kyle replied absent-mindedly. As we walked into the kitchen something caught our attention. "Whoa!" Kyle and I marveled in unison. We were staring at a glowing box the size of my dad's pickup truck. "It's huge!" I gasped. "What is it?" Kyle asked. "It's your house, you should know," I said. "Let's go in it." Kyle said, full of excitement. "No way." I denied. "Please." He begged. "Fine," I gave in, "but if I get hurt, you're paying for the medical bill."

"Creeeeek!" the glowing box's door groaned, "AHHHHHHH!!!" We screamed like little girls as we were sucked into a vortex inside the magical box. We hit the ground with a THUD! "Where are we?" We asked a HUMONGOS man in an Indianapolis Colts jersey. "What do ya mean? You're in the Super Bowl!" He bellowed. "What?" We asked, confused. "Did you guys get concusions? How could you forget you were in the Super Bowl?" He asked us in his deep, and a little annoying voice. "Get out there!" shouted a coach. As we trotted onto the field, we looked at the collossal Jumbotron and saw Kyle and I. "Man, those push-ups have really paid off!" I thought to myself.

But then we saw the score. It was 21-21 with one second left, and the New Orleans Saints had the ball on the 50 yard line. "This is weird, but AWESOME!" I told Kyle. "I know." he replied. "Down. Set. Blue 42 set, HUT," yelled the Saints quarterback, Drew Brees. He dropped back then, threw it deep to his reciever, Marques Coston. I sprinted toward him, leaped into the air, bobbled it, then caught it! I intercepted it! I ran forward, spun away from a lineman, juked out their running back, Reggie Bush, and next thing I knew the only

person between me and sweet sweet victory was a lineman. "Oh great," I thought, "A 6' 375 lbs 30 year old is about to clobber a 4ft8, 70 lbs 10 year old." I braced myself for impact but out of nowhere Kyle knocked him over! I breezed into the endzone and was mobbed by my "teammates." Indianapolis Colts' blue spilt all over the field as we stormed the field. "This may be a weird time to ask, but can I have your autograph." I asked Drew Brees while I was by him. "Wait you're a kid!" He asked me. "Yeah," I replied. "Well, that's embarrassing he blushed.

"How did you block him?" I asked Kyle when I saw him. "I do not know," He grinned.

I will never forget the time I found a magical box and scored the game-winning touchdown in the Super Bowl. In a way, that was like the time I hit the Game-Winning Home Run in the World Series, but that's another story. ☆

Using Varied Sentence Openers
to Create Rhythm and Flow

What Writers Do — In order to keep their readers listening, writers use variation in the way they start their sentences.

What This Writer Does — Efrata uses a wide variety of sentence openers to create fluid movement in her narrative.

Activity for your class:

1. Pass out copies of the story to the students and read the piece together.

2. Ask students to highlight the words or phrases that begin each of the sentences.

3. Take turns reading the sentence beginnings aloud.

4. As a class, brainstorm a list of sentence openers for students to try out in their writing.

Challenge for students:

Choose a piece of writing that you like from your journal or portfolio. In your own piece of writing, try beginning the sentences in different ways. You might use Efrata's beginnings as a bank of ideas to get you started.

Memory Reflection

Where you were	What happened first	What happened next	What happened last	What you thought

I was at my Granpa's lush farm, and that summer day was as hot as a furnace. I was so bored, and the only option I had left was to play with Lottie, my German Sheperd. "Here, girl," I called. Soon enough, Lottie lazily trotted out of the barn, with a few sticks of hay in her silky fur. "You want to explore?" I inquired to the panting dog. Taking slobber drooling down Lottie's mouth as a yes, I skipped down the road, past the black and white cows, towards the forest.

As soon as we reached the outskirts of my grandfather's land, my stomuch lurched. But with Lottie at my heels, I ventured into the forest. The forest was dark and damp. I felt as if millions of eyes were watching my every move. A twig snapped, followed by a faint neigh. In disbelief, I thought, It's just Moonlight and Midnight (horses) in the pasture. Suddenly Lottie growled towards the shadows. "What is it, girl?" I tensely asked. I was answered with a whimper.

I soon decided whatever it was, it was pretty scary. Mustering my bravery, I headed towards the trees. A loud clutter of crows snapped my mind to attention, as I trudged through thorn bushes. As I approached a clearing, what I saw made my eyes as wide as tomatoes.

There right in the clearing, lay a colt. A few rays of sun made the leather brown skin of the colt glow. But what amazed me the most was the large, swollen, right hind leg of the horse. When the horse glanced up, I saw a twisted, pained, expression. Suddenly I saw my grandfather with his horse trailer. Quickly we hauled the injured colt, and made our way back to the farm.

When we got to the farm, me and Lottie inpaticently paced outside the barn door. She'll be okay, I constantly told myself. I was astounded when my grandfather's wrinkled face appeared, and then said "She'll be okay." I heaved a sigh of relief, and headed towards the colt that I had found. I learned that any day can start out dull, but turn out to be the most exciting time of your life. Just like me and my colt. ☆

Using Precise Language to Create Visual Snapshots

What Writers Do — Writers use precise, carefully chosen words to create images in their readers' minds. These images are like visual snapshots that paint a picture for the reader.

What This Writer Does — Elizabeth skillfully uses language to create stunning images that readers can easily visualize.

Activity for your class:

1. Distribute copies of Elizabeth's piece and ask a volunteer to read it aloud.

2. Have students reread the part about the cliffs and highlight the snapshot from, "*I saw some roots...*" to "*...directing her with my left hand.*"

3. Invite students to draw a sketch of the narrator and her friend hanging on to the cliffs.

4. Count how many details in the sketch came from the text.

Challenge for students:

Write an action snapshot using enough detail that someone could draw a picture of the scene, using your description as a guide. Try writing snapshots and adding them to one of your own personal narratives.

Memory Reflection

Where you were	What happened first	What happened next	What happened last	What you thought

In the Cliffs

"EAT MY DUST, SUCKER!" I yelled over my shoulder so Robin could hear me. We darted past Bill's house as if we were gazelles in a stampede.

But Robin just happened to interrupt my thoughts by yelling "NEVER!" Robin and I had started a race. There were strategies racing through my mind of how to get further than she will. Then it hit me! I should run and climb all the way up the cliffs. I had started to climb the cliffs by the time Robin caught up to me. Our little race had become an adventure.

"OW!" I whined. I pricked my finger on a thorn as sharp as a knife. I sucked on it until I got it to stop hurting, then I told Robin "My blood tastes salty." We both couldn't keep from laughing. We started climbing again, but this time with caution. Somehow we managed to get too high for comfort. Robin has always been afraid of heights. I wasn't usually afraid, but this time I was. I looked down to find any footholds, but my eyes snapped shut. I made myself open them again and surveyed the cliff side. I saw some roots shaped like little hoops coming out of the cliff side. I tested my weight on each root. I managed to find a comfortable position holding onto 3 of the roots. My feet were on 2 of them, and I held on to the last one with my right hand. I stood up and helped Robin onto some of the other roots directing her with my left hand. We climbed the rest of the way down the same way we got up. We were back to safety. I looked up to where I was and trembled at the sight. Quickly I checked if Robin was okay. Then I checked if I was okay. It all added up to scraped hands and sore feet. I of course can't forget a spanking from my mom. ☆

Using Foreshadowing to Create Mood

What Writers Do — Writers choose words to create moods, much in the same way that musical composers choose major or minor keys for their songs to create a certain feeling.

What This Writer Does — Near the beginning of his narrative about rescuing a puppy, Jarod skillfully uses language to establish a mood of dread. This mood gives us a clue about what will come next and keeps us engaged in the story.

Activity for your class:

1. Read the piece aloud as students follow along on their copies.

2. Have students reread the piece, highlighting words and phrases that give them a sense that something bad might happen.

3. Have students share their highlighted words with a partner or in a small group and discuss their choices. What do the highlighted words add to the piece?

4. As a class, make a list of the words that set up the mood in Jarod's narrative.

Challenge for students:

Write a piece about something that happened in your life that caused worry or anxiety. Add to your piece the words from the class list or other words and phrases that create a sense of dread and see if you like the mood it creates.

Memory Reflection

Where you were	What happened first	What happened next	What happened last	What you thought

---

Finding Snowball

Sunlight streamed through the clouds as I sprinted after my sister. We were in the movie theaters parking lot, heading back to the car. "Hey wait up," I yelled after my sister. "I am going to beat you," she teased. I put on an extra burst of speed just before she tagged the car. "I beat you, I beat you," she taunted. "I let you win," I muttered just loud enough for her to hear. "No you didn't," she whined. "I beat you." "Whatever," I said under my breath.

A shadow passed over the car. I looked into the sky. The clear day was gone and to take its place were huge, dark, ominous, storm clouds. I stared out the window. My eyes glued to where I'd last seen the sun. Just then I saw a streak of white. It's just my imagination, I thought. Then I heard a squeaking sound, It's just the car I thought, still trying to make out the sun hidden behind the clouds. Next I heard a bloodcurling howl. My mom slammed on the brakes. I stared out into the gloom. There out in the middle of the parking lot was a little white puppy, alone in the darkness howling like it had lost everything in the world.

After Mom got the shivering puppy inside the car, I asked "What should we name it?" My brother and sister eventually started arguing. "What's the problem," I asked. "I want to name it Snow, but Alyssa wants to name it Snow White," my brother said calmly. "I personaly don't like the name Snow White," I said. "But Snow White's a cool name," my sister protested. "How about we just name her Snowball," my mom suggested warily. "Sure," I said, "but how do we know she's a girl?" I asked. "Let me see her," my mom commanded. "I handed her the puppy, as she squeaked in displeasure. "He's a boy," my mom said. "Well I am still calling him Snowball," my brother declared. "Me too," Alyssa agreed. My mom handed him back to me, and suddenly he went limp. I clutched his scrawny body to my chest. "No," I wispered in dismay. I thought hard, and the more I thought about it the more I knew someone had abandoned him, he had no collar and no one who loved their dog would leave him in a parking lot. I imagined it. A man kicking out a little white puppy and driving off, leaving the puppy to fend for itself. Anger boiled inside me, how could someone leave such a cute little puppy like him, I thought. I pressed my ear up against his tiny chest listening for his heart beat. Hearing nothing I pressed my ear deeper into his wiry fur. Then I heard it, the steady beat of his heart, but it was faint.

Dread crept over me as we walked into the vet. I anxiously waited for some news about Snowball. Finally a nurse walked in. Her expression gave nothing away. "Your Mom wants to see you," she said. Snowballs okay, I told myself, he has to be. I walked to the back room, opened the door, and trudged inside. All of the sudden a big furry lump leaped into me almost toppling me over. I looked up to see Snowball staring into my eyes. "We get to keep him," my mom said in a low wisper.

Eventually we got him all the doggy stuff he needed to live a happy doggy life, and he soon settled down to living in a house instead of being on the run. Every time I see his tiny heart beating, I remember the time when those heart beats were limited. Every day I own him, Snowball tackles me, the same way he did at the vet. Though he's not the little scrap we found he's still a very cute puppy. Finding him is the best thing I could ever hope for. ☆

Building Suspense in a Narrative Through Questions and Answers

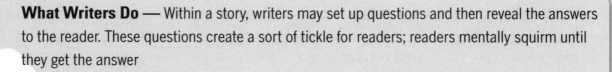
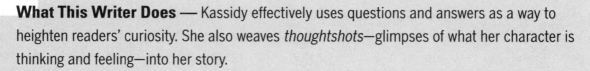

What Writers Do — Within a story, writers may set up questions and then reveal the answers to the reader. These questions create a sort of tickle for readers; readers mentally squirm until they get the answer

What This Writer Does — Kassidy effectively uses questions and answers as a way to heighten readers' curiosity. She also weaves *thoughtshots*—glimpses of what her character is thinking and feeling—into her story.

Activity for your class:

1. Read this story out loud to the class first, then pass out copies.

2. As a class, create a list of questions that the narrator had to answer.
   Examples:
   - Where is Dad?
   - Would Christmas be the same as every other year?
   - Is Dad in the bathroom? Garage? Kitchen?
   - Where is a place we've never been before?
   - Why does he want us to go to the pool in the cold?
   - Where can boys go?

3. Ask students how their favorite stories and movies tap into curiosity and build suspense in a similar way. Share examples together.

Challenge for students:

Write about a time when you were trying to figure out something. Try layering questions and answers into your story to build the reader's curiosity.

Memory Reflection

Where you were	What happened first	What happened next	What happened last	What you thought

"Wake up!" yelled Kamden (my little brother.) "OK! OK!" I yelled back. Right when I started to get up, I remembered that today was Christmas. That meant we might get to do something that we can never do again! When we ran to get dad something was not right. Dad was gone! We split up to see if we could find him. We searched everywhere, the bathrooms, closets, garage, and the kitchen. "Would we ever find our dad? Would we have a Christmas surprise like every other year?" I thought to myself.

I searched the dressers and found a mysterious note. It said, "If you want to find me you should go somewhere you have never been, but before you go put on clothes or you will freeze." "The trees!" we yelled together. We ran to our room and got dressed. We got flashlights because it was still dark out. We raced out the door and headed for the trees. Stuck on a branch was another note.

It said, "Go to the place you started and put on supplies you need for swim lessons and go somewhere else you have been. The code is "Merry Christmas." Say it and push and the gate will open!" "The pool," we yelled together. "You have got to be kidding me!" I thought. It was 45°F degrees outside and he wanted us to put on swimsuits and goggles?" I thought. We ran inside and put on our swim suits and goggles and got our towels. We raced down the street to the pool.

When we got there we said the code and pushed. The gate opened and we saw a note taped on to it. It said, "Go somewhere boys can go but not girls." "The boys bathroom!" Kamden mumbled. We slowly walked to the bathroom and..."surprise!" yelled dad. We stared at dad, "Your surprise is that you get to jump into the pool!" he yelled. I cannot believe he just said that because he is always cold and that he is standing in his bathing suit on Christmas day! I thought. But I can't waste it. So I raced to the pool and jumped in.

It was hot in the pool so I floated on top of the water in peace. Kamden joined me. Dad jumped in and joined us. We laid there for 4 hours straight. We left because we were starving. I was so surprised I kept pinching myself because that day was so surprising.

That morning was full of surprises. I wish we could do that again. It makes me feel warm when I think of that day. That day had a super full pack of surprises! ☆

Using Participles and Participial Phrases

What Writers Do — Writers use participles and participial phrases to pack a lot of information into a small amount of space.

What This Writer Does — Lydia skillfully uses participles and participial phrases in her writing to create descriptive, evocative sentences. These give her piece a sense of fluid movement and rich depth.

Activity for your class:

1. Distribute copies of the piece and read it together as a class.

2. Identify a few participles and participial phrases together as you define and explain these constructions to your students.

   - *Participles* are verbs used as adjectives; they end in –ed or –ing (like *toasted* or *toasting*).

   - *Participial phrases* use additional words (like *toasted in butter*).

3. Have students color-code the participles and participial phrases using highlighters:

   green—one-word participles, such as *stuffed, smouldering, horrifying*

   yellow—participial phrases, such as *bursting into tears, becoming more terrified by the second, thinking about the movie*

Challenge for students:

Take a look at any piece you have written. Have you used participles and participial phrases? Try adding some and notice the difference it makes.

Memory Reflection

Where you were	What happened first	What happened next	What happened last	What you thought

Yellow flames began to lick up the curtains. "Mom, where is Maui?" I inquired frantically. No answer. With the house going up in flames I thought of my stuffed teddy, Maui, about to be burned. I felt like bursting into tears the thought was so horrifying. Becoming more terrified by the second, I rushed around the smouldering house, trying to think of where Maui was. Thoughts flashed through my head like a slideshow on fast. Bedroom, bathroom, kitchen windowsill. I stopped for barely a moment, thinking about how I didn't have much time left to find Maui.

As I dashed towards the kitchen, I thought about the many places where Maui could be. When I reached the kitchen, no type of stuffed animals were in sight. Maybe Mandy stuffed him in one of the cabinets as a joke on me. The thought flashed through my head like a cheetah, fast and gleaming. I started opening and closing cabinets, making whooshing and slamming noises. "What if he has already been devoured by the fire," a little voice inside my head whispered maliciously. This thought worried me. I was so caught up in finding my bear that I never thought about him and his little palm trees becoming a picnic for the roaring wave of red orange flames. I would feed myself to hungry tigers if he burned.

Next I tore around the house looking for my prized possesion. My room was next on the list, so I scurried through inches of ash to find Maui. When I approached my room, one of the beames that held up the doorframe fell. "Oh my goodness, what am I going to do?" I wondered. I moved some of the wood, scattering dust everywhere. "Maybe I should leave this room alone," I thought tearfully. Maui could have been stuck in that ashy tomb.

Soon there was only 1 more place to look. I had checked every place a little bear could be. I stumbled blindly towards the laundry room, praying that this room was his sanctuary. Drops of sweat ran down my face and dribbled off my forehead. One of my toenails was blue and my shoes had fallen off. I had splinters all over my hands and my feet were cut and bruised. But all I cared about was Maui. I slowly opened the door and reached my hand up for the cord to the light. I slowly pulled the string and closed my eyes, ready for the tragic dissapointment of no teddy. I opened one of my eyes a crack and saw a palm tree pattern. "Maui," I thought. "The palm tree you saw was just your imagination," the little voice whispered, "no need to be dissapointed beyond limits." I began to believe the little voice, make it stronger. "Yeah right," I thought, snapping out of my reverie and opening my eyes. And there was Maui plain as day. I grabbed him and started to run.

I escaped from my house just in time. Since then I have gotten many stuffed animals of all kind. I have remembered to love them all but I am glad I found Maui in the nick of time. ☆

Using Variety When Introducing Narrator Thoughts

What Writers Do — Writers include a narrator's thoughts and introduce those thoughts in a variety of ways rather than repeating, "I thought...I thought...I thought...."

What This Writer Does — In this first-person memory piece, Madeleine expertly guides her readers through her experience on the soccer field by revealing her thought processes. To avoid repetition, she weaves in a wide variety of sentence types and starters.

Activity for your class:

1. Read the piece aloud with your class.

2. Ask students to reread it and underline phrases or sentences that reveal the narrator's thoughts.

3. Together, make a list of phrases that show thinking. For example:
   - *What was that supposed to mean?*
   - *I tried to think straight, but...*
   - *I was too busy wondering about...*
   - *I had realized that...*
   - *I was ready to...*
   - *I told myself...*
   - *Now was the time to...*
   - *I know I could...*
   - *I found my inner strength...*

4. Post the class list on the wall for reference throughout the year. Invite students to add to it, selecting other useful phrases from student writing or literature.

Challenge for students:

Try adding some inner monologue to a narrative you are writing. Use a variety of sentence starters. Try using some from the class list.

Memory Reflection

Where you were	What happened first	What happened next	What happened last	What you thought

The Game Plan

1...2...3...ORANGE CRUSH! When I was about to run out to the field, I heard my dad say, "This is it, find your inner strength." What was that supposed to mean? On your mark, get set, GO, but it was too late to ask because we were off to try and win the game.

I tried to think straight and stay focused on the game, but I was too busy wondering about what my dad had told me. Then kick, hit, fall. I was down, hard. I felt like I was having a huge migrain. Everyone rushed over to me and tried to push me up. They had no trouble doing that, because I had realized that I had lost my wigly tooth and I got up myself. I was furious. That's when I found my inner strength! People kept asking me if I wanted to sit out on the bench, but I said, "No." I had gotten this far, I was ready to get my game on. With almost no time on the clock, I intercepted the soccer ball. Kids on my team were screaming for me to pass the ball, but I had told myself, "No." I had found my inner strength and now was the time to use it. I faked a pass to the right and then dribbled the ball left past the defenders. Then it was just me and the goalie.

I turned around just in time to see a lot a bigger kids running toward me. I decided it was my time to shine. I did not pass to the left or the right, I kicked the ball straight into the net and over the goalie. Yippy! I had made the winning goal! I swiftly ran over to my dad and hugged him. "I knew I could to it," I whispered. "I found my inner strength." ☆

Using Metaphor to Illuminate a Life Lesson

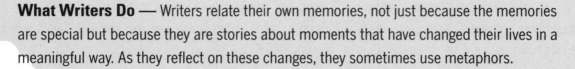

What Writers Do — Writers relate their own memories, not just because the memories are special but because they are stories about moments that have changed their lives in a meaningful way. As they reflect on these changes, they sometimes use metaphors.

What This Writer Does — As she writes about the memories she has of her uncle's funeral, Maria uses an extended metaphor to illuminate the lesson she learned about life. This adds depth to her writing and invites readers to reflect on events in their own lives.

Activity for your class:

1. Have students follow along on their copies while you read the piece aloud.

2. Reread the extended metaphor, from *"Life is a maze"* to the end.

3. Discuss all the ways that the author extends this metaphor.
   Examples:

   - *She explains how life is like a maze.*
   - *She describes how the maze can slow you down.*
   - *She tells what stops you and traps you in the maze.*
   - *She tells what happens when you find your way out of the maze.*

Challenge for students:

Try writing a metaphor for life. Start with "Life is a…" and then see how many ways you can extend the metaphor. Then incorporate it into a personal narrative that you are writing, or use the text structure below to write a new one.

Memory Reflection

Where you were	What happened first	What happened next	What happened last	What you thought

Always and Forever

The suspense grew. I was on the edge of the sofa, my eyes glued to the T.V. screen. He pulled the lever. Rrring! The shrill screech of the phone interupted the movie. Aw, man! I thought. Who could it be? Daddy spoke for an extreme amount of time. When he finally hung up he spoke only three words. "Ernest has died."

My focus was no longer on the movie. No! This couldn't be happening. I knew my Uncle Ernest was very sick but I didn't think he would die! I thought about watching the movie. Should I be doing this or comforting my Aunt Margret? I ran upstairs when the movie ended and jumped into my bed weeping softly.

When I woke up, three weeks had passed. I don't remember waking up, but I must have because I had different P.J.'s on (NO I don't sleepwalk). 21 days had passed and today Uncle Ernest was having his funeral. I dreaded the moment with every move I made. I knew I would cry really loud and I didn't want to. I would have to be strong, I told myself. As I climbed into the car I built up my courage, stacking it up like wooden blocks. It was off to the funeral.

In the three rows of chairs at the front I saw Aunt Margret. (Uncle Ernest was her husband.) I tried to get to her, but the crowd of Aunts, Uncles, cousins, and even pets was too thick. Someone started to say something and everyone got quiet, and so did I.

As the speech ended, I watched the box with my Uncle go down into a hole. It was a sad, but beautiful moment. Mixed emotions flooded my body. I was glad that he was in a better place, depressed that he was gone, overjoyed that he was watching over me, and many other feelings. I stood like a panther, silent and waiting.

"Your uncle made this. I want you to have it," Aunt Margret's eyes were red and teary as she handed it to me. She pushed a heart-shaped box into my hands. I opened it and saw that inside was a wood ornament. A bunny peered over the wooden wreath. I smiled and whispered, "It's beautiful! I'll treasure it forever." As she walked away I thought, I've learned an important lesson today. Life is a maze. You are always finding new halls to explore. Your emotions guide you around, showing you new doors to open. Sometimes your feelings don't feel so good and you slow down. You may even stop! When this happens you need to get back on track. Mourning is a big stopper. Mourning should not BE your life, but only a part of it, otherwise you will stay in the same hall forever. When you find your way out of the maze (when you die) you start a new maze. I think that the key to the happiness hall is never stopping (A.K.A. mourning ALL THE TIME) otherwise you may never make it. ☆

Writing Observations

What Writers Do — Writers practice using their powers of observation in many different ways. Even when they are writing about an object, they heighten readers' interest by writing about what they see, what they notice, what they suspect, and what they can tell about the object.

What This Writer Does — Rachel focuses on a bone, explaining what it looks like, how she reaches it, and what she sees and thinks when she examines it closely.

Activity for your class:

1. Read this piece together with the class.

2. Have students reread the piece, highlighting every thought that the author has about the bone.

3. Read the piece aloud without the highlighted parts and discuss the difference it makes when those sections are removed.

Challenge for students:

Write about an object you've found (or been given). As you write, try to do what Rachel did: Observe the object closely and describe what you see and what you notice and suspect about it.

Memory Reflection

Where you were	What happened first	What happened next	What happened last	What you thought

The Coolest Bone Ever

Vroom, vroom went my blue, baby bear four wheeler. My sister and I were off looking for bones. I had driven around the forty acre field about fifty-two times on my dad's ranch. Right before I was about to give up and go home I spotted a dirty, white, and old bone. I drove over to get a better look. My sister got a better look first and when she saw what type of bone it was. She screamed a blood curling scream! I jumped in my seat when I heard her scream! I drove a little closer to see myself what kind of bone it was.

Soon I had driven as far as I could. The bone was surrounded by cactus. I jumped off the four wheeler. "Ow!" I yelled as a big, long thorn pierced my skin when I jumped off. It hurt as bad as having your foot run over by a fourteen wheeler! It hurt so bad but that was not what I was thinking about. I was thinking about how to get that huge bone. First, I decided I would back up and stand on the top of the four wheeler seat. Next, I would look for an easy path to get to the bone. Then, when I found a path I hopped down and ran over or jumped across whatever was in my way to get that bone. When I finally reached I picked it up and examened it. I could tell that it was very old and that it hadn't been touched in a long time. Also I could tell it was a skeleton bone. As I started to walk back I saw Gabby was very nerves. When I reached the four wheeler Gabby exclaimed nervesly, "Are you really going to take that bone home?" "Yeah," I replied as I hopped on the four wheeler.

The whole way I had to listen to ew ew. I was so annoyed with my dumb sister. I couldn't stand it one more minute, so I turned around and told her to be quite and that I don't like to ride with big fat babies. After that, she was extremely quiet the whole way to my special spot. When we reached my spot I jumped off quickly to set down my newly found bone with all my other special bones I had found. I thought this was the coolest bone I have ever found. Whenever I see a skeleton bone or any other regular bone I think of the time my sister and I found the coolest bone ever found in this world. Do you think you'll ever find a cooler bone? ☆

Adding Rich Dialogue to a Narrative

What Writers Do — Writers create dialogue to bring a story to life. Through it, we can hear the voice of the narrator and other characters, which adds realism, voice, and action to a narrative.

What This Writer Does — Sarah expertly weaves dialogue into her story as she recounts her first day on a new campus, combining this element with action and thoughts to create a recounting of her day that is easy for the reader to see, hear, and experience.

Activity for your class:

1. Distribute copies and read the piece with the class. Have students use highlighters to color-code the chunks of text:

   - pink—speech
   - green—action
   - yellow—narrator thoughts

2. Discuss how this piece would be different if any one of the three colors were left out.

Challenge for students:

Add some dialogue to a narrative you have written. Color-code it the same way. Is one color missing? Think about what you can add so that your colors are as balanced as Sarah's.

Memory Reflection

Where you were	What happened first	What happened next	What happened last	What you thought

As I walked into the double-doors of my brand new school, I thought, here I go this is it, new school new life, I'm starting over. I was dissapointed in my parents. I thought, Why did I have to transfer to another school, why couldn't I stay at Hexter? This question echoed through my mind all summer, but every time I asked my parents, I got the same answer "So that you can make new friends." My parents would say. As I walked further down the hall, I spotted a girl, about my age, kneeling to the ground with a huge pile of papers surrounding her.

I ran over to the girl and said "Need any help," in my most polite voice. "Sure, thanks," she said back shyly. While we were picking up the papers, I couldn't help but stare at her blue, glistening eyes. When we finished picking up the papers, I handed her the ones I had picked up. "My name's Sarah," I said to her in a friendly voice, "I'm new here." "Me too, my names Exene," she in amazement. As we shook hands the bell rang. "What class are you in?" I asked Exene.

"4B," she replied as she jogged to class. I could tell she was in a rush. I quickly glanced at the card that I got in the mail. "Me too! Can you show me the way?" I questioned. "Sure follow me," she said back.

I realized that Exene may actually be my friend.

When we got into class I saw middle-aged woman with streaks of gray hair. She looked a little strict. So just in case she was, I kept my mouth shut. Where we were supposed to sit there were sticky notes. I peered in the second row and saw SARAH then next to me I saw EXENE. We sat down at the same time. Then, Mrs. Hall, our teacher passed out a sheet on homophones. About 15 minutes later, we had to go to specials. We walked over to the gym to play dodge-ball. And of course I was on the same team as Exene. When specials was over, we went back to class for S.S.R. A few hours later, we went to lunch. I sat next to Exene, and together we talked, and laughed hysterically. Then it was time for recess. Exene, a bunch of other kids, and I all played tag.

Finally it was the end of the day. Outside when we were waiting for our parents, Exene and I exchanged phone numbers. "Wanna be best friends," she whispered to me in a shy voice. "Ya sure that would be great!" I squealed.

"How was your first day of school," my mother questioned me. "Guess what, guess what, guess what!" I shouted. "I made a new friend." That day I learned that when you are opened to new friends there are many possibilities. ☆

Writing From the Point of View of a Fictional Character

What Writers Do — Writers sometimes create fictional narrators to give a new voice to their ideas.

What This Writer Does — Ashley speaks as an 86-year-old woman faced with a difficult decision. This character is remarkably believable because of Ashley's carefully chosen details, which enable the reader to "slip into the skin" of the narrator.

Activity for your class:

1. Distribute copies of the piece and read it aloud with your students.

2. Ask them to reread it, highlighting the words and phrases that show that this narrator is much older than the author.

3. Share and discuss the highlighted sections, first with partners or groups and then with the whole class.

Challenge for students:

Practice writing from the point of view of a fictional narrator by retelling the same incident from the point of view of Annibell, Devon, or Margarete and see how it changes.

OR

Write a new story of your own with a fictional narrator who is older (or younger) than you are.

The Story of My Thinking

I used to think...	But this happened...	So now I think...

Pain and Pride

At a young age I was taught that pain helped build character. I was also told that it was okay to be prideful, but now in my "advanced age," as people like to call it, I have learned different. I'm at the tender age of 86 now and I know a thing or two about pain. I've delt with pain all my life, but I had never encountered any amount of pain near the measure I felt when my children came to me and proclaimed it was my time to join a nursing home. My heart was crushed. I felt like a bug on the bottom of some fat man's size 13. It nearly killed me to think my children had conspired against me in such a way. They believed I would be safer there. My youngest, Annibell, showed me the statistics of the increasing number of colored women dying from stroke and heart attacks. Maybe the statistics were true and maybe I would be safer at a retirement home but I was not going to let some silly statistics tell me where I should live and die. I wasn't going anywhere. For the next few months my children would hound me with information regarding my health and would constantly ask if I was going to move. My answer never changed it was always no. Every time I answered they would give me a look of sadness and regretfully change topic. One day, a few weeks later, I recieved a letter in the mail from my closest friend's family. It read:

Dear Charlene,

We regret to tell you this but Margarete Daniels has passed away. The doctors say it was a heart attack that lead to her sudden death. We hope you will join us at her funeral next Sunday.

With love,

The Daniels

I was shocked by the tragic news I learned from the letter. Margarete was younger than I was when she passed and looked fit as a fiddle. It brought my heart to tears to think I would never see her, talk to her or even see her smile again. At her funeral my family and I could be seen sobbing over her once joyous body, but as we proceded to leave the services my middle child, Devon, came to me and once again asked if I would join a nursing home. I took a slight glance to where Margarete lay in her cascet and then turned back to my son. With a sour face but love in my eyes I told him that I would go anywhere if it meant I could have more time to spend with my children and all my beautiful grand-babies. Later that next week I was in room 309 at Neches Care Center. My children and their children would come by and visit me every other day. The days I have spent with my family are precious and I hope to remember them forever. I hate when I am wrong even though I truly feel I am right, but I should have never let the thought of my pain or my pride stand in the way of me making a life changing decision. ☆

Using Variations of "Said"

What Writers Do — Writers use words with subtle differences when writing dialogue, employing wide ranges of choices to convey their thoughts to their readers. This keeps the writing from becoming repetitive and boring.

What This Writer Does — In this touching memory about losing a beloved pet, Elizabeth uses rich, textured language choices instead of the word "said."

Activity for your class:

1. Read the piece together with your class, or invite a student volunteer to read as others follow along.

2. Assign partners or groups to go through the piece together, looking for dialogue.

3. Ask them to highlight all the variations of "said" or "asked" *(replied, questioned)* and all of the verb phrases (like *"solemnly reported"*) that go with each line of dialogue.

4. Make a class word wall of these responses as student groups share. Title it "Talking Words," "Better than Said," or something your class comes up with. Add to it during the year.

Challenge for students:

Find a memory piece you have written or write a new one using the text structure below. Add dialogue if needed and revise using the words from the wall chart.

Memory Reflection

Where you were	What happened first	What happened next	What happened last	What you thought

My Little Abby

The scent of her fur still surrounds my nose. The image of her floppy brownish ears remains in my brain. The pain from knowing she didn't have to die still dwells in my broken heart. I remember every detail of the day Abby was put to sleep. She was about 10 years old, and I was 15…

"Gene! What's wrong with Abby?" Lucy interrogated as she examined the miniature dachshund stretched out across the kitchen and into the living room carpet! I scurried across the kitchen and into the living room while finishing my last bite of toaster stroodle. Lucy glanced up at me to reveal her tensed green eyes. My brown eyes shifted from Lucy to Abby. "I don't know," I answered.

"Momma, it's Abby," I said impatiently. "What's wrong with Abby?" she moaned. "Come look, please." I suggested as I gestured her to the living room. Mom slowly slid the covers off of her and pulled herself out of bed. Her short, brown hair was still neat and clean, and her legs were slim and tan. Her eyes were deep hazel. She glanced at the chubby dog who was draped across the carpet. "I think she's sick," Mom mumbled, still exhausted from the busy summer week. "What time is it?" she questioned me. I glanced at the clock. "11:00 A.M," I replied. My mom took another look at Abby. "Let's go get dressed and see what's wrong," she demanded. I slid my lengthy fingers through my straight, long blonde hair. Then I shuffled to my room and changed out of my pajamas into my denim shorts and brown tank top. I threw my hair up into a loose ponytail, and headed out to the white suburban.

"Honestly don't know what to say," Dr. Cullins solemnly reported. "Your dog has a rare disease. I'm very sorry to inform you that the disease is fatal." My whole world nearly stopped when I heard his words. Lucy, Mom, and I were not only shocked but devastated. Lucy was probably shocked the most out of all 3 of us. She was only 9; she didn't understand that dogs didn't live forever, especially Abby. Dr. Cullins sympathized. "The dog is suffering. The best that I can recommend is that you put her to sleep," he painfully suggested. Tears flooded my eyes. My heart skipped a beat. My mom silently bawled. "Gene, you decide. She's your dog," Lucy suggested. Her curly brown maine was matted up from shaking her head in denial of the news. I turned my head to Doctor Collin. I knew Abby was in pain. I wanted what was best for her, but I couldn't bare the thought of living without her. I strode over to Abby and kissed her beautiful auburn fur. Abby licked my shoulder. I walked over to Dr. Cullins. "Put her to sleep." I sobbed.

I think I did what was right. Now, Abby is gone, but I will never forget my little Abby. ☆

Using Depth and Detail to "Explode" a Moment

What Writers Do — Writers usually narrate their stories sequentially, telling readers what happened first, second, and third, but they don't always dedicate the same number of words to each part.

What This Writer Does — Cady "explodes" an important moment in this lively memory piece, giving readers a chance to experience that moment down to every last detail.

Activity for your class:

1. Holding a remote control as a prop, explain to students that writers choose where they want the reader to focus in a piece; some moments are slowed down, "exploded," told in greater detail (like hitting the "pause" on a remote so you can look more closely). Other moments get less attention (like fast-forwarding through less important scenes).

2. Invite partners to read the piece together.

3. Ask students to circle and discuss the exploded moment—the "I do" moment in the author's dream (*the last half of the second paragraph*).

4. Then have them compare this moment to the real-life "I do" moment (*the end of the third paragraph*).

5. Discuss: How does the "exploded" moment set up the reader for the funny action in the real-life moment? What would've been lost if the dream moment had not contained all of the details it did?

Challenge for students:

Look at a memory piece you have written. Choose a moment to explode and add depth and detail to that moment to bring it to life for the reader.

Memory Reflection

Where you were	What happened first	What happened next	What happened last	What you thought

I Thought I Was Right

Oohs and ahhs fluttered through the room of girls as my Aunt Sara let everyone gaze upon her beautiful new wedding gown. It sparkled under the florescent white light of the church. She handed the dress back to her mother and she then carefully placed it on a hanger, and hung it on the door. Then after chatting and snacking we all eagerly scurried to our places and began rehearsing. Everyone was excited except Aunt Sara who kept repeating her vows over and over. My mother walked up to her and said, "You'll be fine," in a hushed tone. My mother had read the vows to me so many times that I knew them by heart, so if a six-year-old could remember them then she definitely could.

After rehearsal my mom took me to Sonic and we chowed down too. After eating so much, I got really tired so I went straight to bed. My dreams that night were so vibrant and real that for a little while I thought they actually were real. I also had not just one dream, but many and they were all about the wedding, except one little bitty thing; I was Aunt Sara! I was standing at the alter looking at the person I absolutely loved, so much so that I would agree to marry him, and I couldn't say anything! It was like I had gone completely blank. My eyes teared as I felt every single pair of eyes locked on me as they awaited for my words to escape through my mouth. I wanted to scream, "Yes, I do, forever and always!" at the top of my lungs, but no matter how hard I tried, I couldn't.

I woke up the next morning full of confidence about my Aunt Sara, because if she couldn't say it, I was going to say it for her. Being the sly six-year-old I was, I didn't tell anyone of my ingenious plan to save the wedding, that way no one could steal my idea. So I went about the rest of my day preparing myself for the wedding and calculating every little detail of my plan. At 2:00 pm everyone was in their places and ready to go. I gave Aunt Sara a final hug and then "The Wedding March" started. We both walked down the aisle and I watched and waited as she exchanged her vows. When it was time to say "I do" she froze, just as I thought. "I do," I exclaimed. Everyone laughed and Aunt Sara said, "You're right kiddo. I do."

At the reception, I danced with everyone and they could not stop talking about me saying, "I do." When it was my turn to dance with Aunt Sara, she thanked me and said I knew just what to say, so I said, "Yeah, I thought I was right." Then we both laughed and finished our fairytale ending, at least until the next day. ☆

Showing How a Character Changes

What Writers Do — Writers reveal change in a narrative. The more the writer shows levels of change, the more rich and satisfying the reading is. This change is the key to creating characters that are dynamic, not static.

What This Writer Does — In this personal piece, Cecelia brilliantly tracks not only the action but also the changes in the narrator's emotions that occur in the midst of the action and the change in her that results from the experience. This adds depth to her character and interest for the reader.

Activity for your class:

1. Pass out copies of the piece and read it aloud.

2. Have students track the changes in the narrator's confidence level using different colored highlighters:

    *   pink—no confidence
    *   yellow—some confidence
    *   green—full of confidence

Challenge for students:

Think of a moment in your life when something happened that made you feel a strong emotion. Use the text structure below to write a personal narrative about your experience. Include your emotions and, like Cecelia did, show how your feelings changed—and how you did. When you are finished, step back to see if a reader could color-code your piece and see the change in you.

Memory Reflection

Where you were	What happened first	What happened next	What happened last	What you thought

"Ugh! Come on guys hustle after that loose ball. I am pretty sure it's not going to come to you automatically." Coach Terri said scornfully. "You're out here to get better, not stay the same."

I am so glad it's summer so I can do my favorite thing anytime I want, playing basketball! I go to ACU Basketball camp every summer and I enjoy the work-outs and stuff, but last year I faced something controversial. "Gosh, it's been a long day," I complained to my friend Emily. "Tell me about it!" she replied. It was only our first day and it was already tough. I thought, I hope I can make it two more days! "Beep!" The whistle sounded. "All right girls, come and sit in the center of the court." Coach Shawna stated. "Today we are going to isolate you into teams by your athleticism.

"Wow, looks like we got a great team!" Emily said. All I could do was smile because I figured out I was the only junior high girl, and the rest were in high school. I was happy at first until I realized I had to play against other high school girls too! I was in a giant state of shock, because our first game was at two o'clock this afternoon and it was nearly twelve. As my team and I were putting on our basketball shirts, shoes, and braces I could feel my heart beating out of my chest. Everytime I looked up, all I saw were bigger girls which made me feel like a small wimp!

"Okay, we need the Shooting Angels to come down to warm up, you have one hour!" Great that was us! We were playing against the Shooting Bullets, which I heard had an awesome team that hasn't lost, but we are undefeated as well. "Hey Cecelia, come over here for a second." Coach Terri yelled. "Before you say anything Coach, I need to tell you something. I don't think I can hang with these girls. They're too big and tough for me," I replied.

"You see I knew you were going to tell me that, but I have news for you. Cecelia I wouldn't put you on the highest level if I knew you couldn't do it. Just because you're not as tall as them doesn't mean you're not good. So go out there and win!"

"All right let's get this game started," Coach Shawna retorted. I couldn't believe I was starting in the game. Looking in the crowd of people I found my parents, happy as ever cheering for me! I was guarding a girl maybe two inches taller than me so it wasn't that bad. I was doing better than I thought I was going to do. It was the second quarter and the score was twenty-three to eighteen, we were up, but then a girl named Mallory who was at least six feet tall, started scoring over Emily. I was praying that Coach Terri wouldn't tell me to switch with Emily, but it happened anyways. It was in the middle of the third quarter when I figured out how to block this beast! All I had to do was put my hands straight up because she was afraid to shoot over someone. Unfortunetly, the Bullets caught up from the previous shots. The score was tied with twenty-six, in the fourth quarter with fifty seconds left. I was bringing the ball down and I called for an isolation, and did a fake to my left, switched hands and did a reverse lay-up. "Bzzz!!!" The scoreboard buzzed with zero time left! The Shooting Angels won with a clean victory. I was extatic and I really did surprise myself, because I was actually able to stick with those gigantic girls! Now I definitely can't wait till next summer for another tricky challenge! ☆

Using Introspection in a Memoir

What Writers Do — Writers often incorporate self-reflection into personal narratives. Sometimes this includes commentary about their attitudes and how they have changed over time.

What This Writer Does —In her reflective personal narrative about a near-fatal choice she made as a 4-year-old, Cristina includes commentary about her attitudes then and now and closes the piece with an insightful culminating statement.

Activity for your class:

1. Pass out copies of the piece and read it aloud with your students.

2. Ask students to do the following:
   - Highlight in green any words or phrases that reveal the attitudes of the 4-year-old.
   - Highlight in yellow any words or phrases that reveal the attitudes held by the narrator's older self.
   - Discuss the changes you see.

3. Circle the message that is a life lesson for people of all ages.

Challenge for students:

Look at a personal narrative you have written. See what happens if you add some attitudes you had at a younger age and compare them to your attitudes nowadays.

Or you might want to write a new narrative using the text structure below.

Memory Reflection

Where you were	What happened first	What happened next	What happened last	What you thought

Water Dangers

Regardless of my age, I thought that I could achieve anything and everything there was to achieve. My days were numbered as a youngster and I decided to follow through with my foolish four year old plan.

Growing up as a young toddler, I believed that I could do anything my most beloved cartoon characters would attempt. I once had multiple dreams that I could jump off skyscrapers hundreds of feet tall, fight off evil dwarfs with my one of a kind Barbie ribbon tangler, and even take flight to Toys R' Us to rule as Queen Suzie. I spent long hours preparing for the arch enemy of Batman and Robin to lunge from beneath my twin-sized bed and make me one of their own. I guess you could say that I was one action-packed child with many wild and spectacular dreams. One dream I planned after watching an episode of Scooby-Doo when he made a run for it, and plunged into the deep, shivering sea water. That one episode inspired me and left my parents regretting that they ever allowed me to watch TV shows. Specifically cartoons.

* * *

One hot summer day my family had planned to take a trip to the most popular water park in town: Schliterban. Everyone was excited, packed, and ready to go. We climbed in the mini-van and we were on our way. As my family and I drove through town to reach our destination, I thought of all the exciting and thrilling rides and slides. There were many choices to pick from and I chose one: the normal, plain, old swimming pool. Yes! This year, outgrowing my toddler years, I will leap off the diving board with all my might and dive into the ten foot deep water. The rush of the cold water against my developing, microscopic body would set all my wildest dreams free and I could do it with no problem or hesitation. At least that's what I thought because after all…I'm always right.

We arrived at the water park and there, right in front of me, lay the designer beach chairs, tubes, and a little to the left, mounted to the concrete, the diving board was placed. I slowly crept away from my parents as they payed our way in, then as soon as I was out of sight, I fled towards the diving board. Ignoring all safety precautions, I climbed the steps leading to the top, scanned the perimeter, and was traveling south directly into the deepest part of the water. Bam! I slammed into the water with the cold rush as amazing as I thought it would be, and looked up dazzled at the sight. But then, all of a sudden, I was lifeless. I couldn't swim to the top and the last I had heard were the screams of my name being called out by my parents. I…. was….out.

I regret my foolish plan to this day, but I now have the ability to swim in deep water, and make the decision of whether I'm right or wrong. Infants, Toddlers, teens, adults, we still have so much to learn about ourselves and so much to change about ourselves. ☆

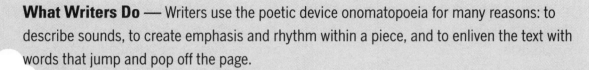

Using Onomatopoeia as an Organizational Device

What Writers Do — Writers use the poetic device onomatopoeia for many reasons: to describe sounds, to create emphasis and rhythm within a piece, and to enliven the text with words that jump and pop off the page.

What This Writer Does — Flor uses onomatopoeia not only to add sound details but also to punctuate—and call attention to—the three different parts of her narrative. The three words *Bang, Pow, Zoom!* structure her piece.

Activity for your class:

1. Pass out copies of the piece and read it aloud.

2. Ask students to look at the three words in the title (*Bang, Pow, Zoom!*) and then find and highlight these words where they appear in the body of the piece.

3. Have students write a summary sentence for each of the three sections that begin with these words.

4. Discuss the effect of using onomatopoeia as an organizational strategy.

Challenge for students:

Look at something you have written, or think about a memory you could turn into a personal narrative. See if you can come up with three (or more) onomatopoeic words that you could use to organize your piece.

OR

As a class, use the text structure below to create a new narrative that matches the structure of Flor's piece. Use onomatopoeia in the three middle sections of your piece, as shown in the model.

Memory Reflection With Onomatopoeia

	(Bang)	(Pow)	(Zoom)	
Where you were	What happened first	What happened next	What happened last	What you thought

Bang, Pow, Zoom

Bang! There was an echo that sounded like someone had just hit their foot on a piece of metal.

"Oww!" screamed Jemma. "That hurts, I don't think I can run in the race, you'll have to put in someone else to run for me, Coach," she stated as a bruise formed on her foot. It was about five minutes before the race started and we needed to find a substitute quickly.

"OK, Celeste come here, we need you to fill in for Jemma, she hurt her foot and can't race today," the Coach explained quickly before the race started.

"I'll fill in for her and do my very best, Coach," I exclaimed.

As I lined up with the other people who were competing, I was ready to beat everyone. I looked down at the black, hot, rubber tar track and thought to myself, Speed I am Speed. There was a little breeze that came with the beautiful weather we had today. It wasn't as bad as after school practice when it was burning hot.

Pow! The noise of the gun was loud and the competitors started running as quickly as they could. Luckily for me I was ready to run and as soon as I heard the gun shot I ran as fast as I could go.

When everyone was running, I was in fifth place going at a steady pace. I had a plan figured out to win this race, it had been planned for weeks and I saved it for today. I would run at a steady pace and slowly speed up as I got closer to the finish line.

It had gotten hot when the sun came out and made it difficult to run on the hot track with your feet feeling like they're on fire. I started getting tired when I began my third lap, but pushed myself to finish. It was challenging because my body was telling me to stop, but I kept going.

I was on my fourth lap, almost done with my heart beating quickly, and I knew I could do this, so I kicked it up a notch. I sped up so I could get in front of everybody else. It was between me and someone from another town in this black and monster green colored track suit. We were both so close to the finish line and...ZOOM! I ran right past her, she looked to the side and saw this black and gold and yellowish suit fly by as if she was on the ground and a car going 100mph zoomed right by her.

"Yea!" the Coach and everyone in the crowd yelled. They were excited I got first place and started crowding around me. My parents were getting emotional. They hugged me and looked at the medal I got. It was gold with a running shoe with wings and a number one trophy planted on the medal.

I embraced the fact that I got first place even though it was challenging, and I couldn't believe it, but I worked for it. This may not be the last race I'm going to be in, so watch your back, competitors. ☆

Using a Story to Illustrate a Life Lesson

What Writers Do — Writers sometimes tell a story in order to illustrate a life lesson for the reader.

What This Writer Does — In this piece, Jenna explains how something scary becomes less scary once she gets more information, or how people are afraid of things they don't understand. She chooses to show this point through narrative rather than directly "preach it."

Activity for your class:

1. Discuss Aesop's fables with the class, pointing out how they all include a moral at the end of the story, also called a truism or life lesson.

2. Tell students that you're going to read a piece aloud, and they should try to think of a life lesson that could go at the end to summarize Jenna's point.

3. Read Jenna's story aloud as students follow along on copies.

4. Ask students to write down on sticky notes what they think the moral of this tale might be.

5. Compare responses by posting them on a class chart. Discuss.

6. Explain that this is one way to find a theme of a piece you are reading; it can also be an effective way to convey advice in a piece you are writing.

Challenge for students:

Write a piece in which you (or your narrator) experience a life lesson. Look at Jenna's ending as a model for your ending.

OR

Write about a time when you learned from a mistake. Explain how it helped you grow as a person.

Memory Reflection

Where you were	What happened first	What happened next	What happened last	What you thought

Just My Imagination

I sighed contently, gazing at the dancing orange flames that licked at the wood. The fire's flames also reflected off of the focus of my fellow campers. It was here that I spent most of my summer—at Uncle Buddy's camp for kids. All of a sudden, my camp councelor, Mrs. Joyce, arose, breathing in the deep scent of pine. She clapped her hands with a bright grin on her face, "Now it's time to tell ghost stories. Who would like to go first?" She held up our homemde story stick. Red-haired Angela Carter grabbed at it and immediately started her gruesome tale. Her story was about a huge monster with the fangs of a wolf that dwells in a lake near here and roams the woods, looking for food. It was said that at every half-moon, he came out.

Hannah, a little blond girl I befriended on the way here, wrapped her arms around me, teeth chattering. I patted her head reassuringly, but looked up to see that tonight was a half-moon. As the night wore on, more stories were told but they weren't nearly as scary as Angela's. In about an hour, the younger kids were yawning and it was time for bed.

I bunked with Hannah and two other girls, Elizibeth and Katie. Snuggling down in my sleeping bag, I stared at the twirling fireflies out of our cabin window. Just then, a shadow dashed in front of the window with a growl and it seemed to be scratching harshly at the wall of the cabin. I shrieked with terror and scrambled away. "What is it now?" complained Katie with impatience in her tone. Elizibeth turned on the light and frowned. "There was a monster out there!" I explained to them, "Just like the one in Angela's story!" Hannah hid under her pink covers and whimpered. Katie just snickered, "You can't possibly be afraid of the dark."

"I promise!" I stated, my blood boiling. "I saw it!" We just left it at that and decided to check for signs of the monster in the morning. I transfered to a bunk away from the window. That night I slept soundly but it seemed like I never really fell asleep. I just knew that the monster was out there. The other girls just didn't see it for themselves. The sun's rays blinded me when I woke up the next morning and it felt like butterflies flew into my stomach. Katie and Elizibeth were dressed and ready, reporting that Hannah was starving and had already gone to breakfast. I nodded as Katie led the way to the back of the cabin. We spread out, looking for clues. Katie came up to me when Elizibeth had dissappeared into the woods. "I'm sorry about last night. I shouldn't have been like that," she said slowly. I forgave her and then heard Elizibeth cry out. Katie and I jogged towards the sound of her voice and saw Elizibeth kneeling on the dry grass. Shoe prints and wheel barrow marks were imprinted on the ground.

All three of us knew the mystery had been solved. After some figuring, we realized it had been Mrs. Joyce using a wheelbarrow to tote water for the fire to be put out. The scratching had just been a tree limb swaying against the window.

I guess I had been wrong even though it had seemed so real. The monster story had been on my mind all night and so my imagination had gotten the better of me. I apologized to Hannah, Elizibeth, and Katie for waking them up at that late hour and for making them scared too. In the end, I knew it was just my imagination. ☆

Combining Action and Back-Story

What Writers Do — Writers may weave several interesting story elements together to create a unique reading experience.

What This Writer Does — Judith combines snapshots, back-story, action, and description to create an exciting adventure story with a great cliffhanger.

Activity for your class:

1. Pass out copies and read the piece together with your class.

2. Have students color-code the piece with highlighters:
   - green—action taking place in the present
   - yellow—back-story or background information (for example, *why the narrator is here, what she is doing, the legend*)

3. Discuss the many ways that this writer embedded important back-story information into the action. (for example, *through dialogue, thoughts, details of the legend*)

Challenge for students:

Write an adventure story, weaving in a back-story. You might want to add a cliffhanger like Judith did, which could lead to a sequel. Check out the text structure below.

A Completely Made-Up Story With Cliffhanger for Sequel

Characters doing something	Problem arises	How they try to solve it	How they solve it	A new problem

---

My eyes focused on my newest discovery. This one I knew for sure would make TIME Magazine. My thoughts flashed back to this morning. I'd woken up at five o'clock to take college students hiking on Elk Mountain in Montana. I was the leading archaeologist, and today we were looking for the Lost Cave with the Iron Door. This was my twenty-sixth hike and I was starting to get discouraged that it was a myth. Even though I felt ninety percent sure it was real. I'd researched it all my life, but finding it was the hard part. We were half way up the mountain when out of the corner of my eye I saw something glimmering in the sun. I waved my hand for the college students to stop. I then ran over to investigate. For a moment I couldn't believe my eyes, for years I had searched for this. Everyone told me it wasn't real but that was going to change.

"What is it?" the students asked.

"This," my quaking voice stated, "is the Lost Cave with Iron Door. It is said to disappear for decades at a time and then reappear again." I ran my fingers over the rusted metal before continuing the rest of the story. "There is a legend that at one point in time there was a gang of robbers and they used this cave to store their loot and as a hide out. These robbers were very successful, in their time they stole hundreds or thousands of dollars of gold. Now that gold would be worth millions or even billions of dollars." I paused for a moment to let the information sink in. "The only problem is that this cave's loot is said to be guarded by the robbers' ghosts, so if you spot the cave you can't leave it or the ghosts will take it away."

Ready to get to work I asked for a pick to pry open the door. Using all my strength the door's hinges wouldn't budge as though they were new. It ended up taking four people to help pry off the lock. The door opened slowly with an eery creek. One of the students handed me a flashlight. When I turned it on my eyes were blinded by flashes of lights from pyramids, stacks, and mountains of gold. I dared myself to take a step through the gold maze. I reflected back on the years I'd spent hiking this mountain, studying the legends, researching other finds that were never proven right until now.

Once out of the cave my students started to carefully bring out the gold while I called the dean of the University. He was very proud, though whenever I made a discovery he always told me, "When a challenge is done there is always another one." He continued to say that he would contact TIME Magazine and the local news. I hung up and started helping the students.

While I was carrying gold bars the ground started to shake violently. I dropped the gold and quickly ran for the door but it was too late. It had bolted shut with me, alone, in it. Trapped in the dark I searched for my flashlight. I felt around finding it next to a pile of gold. I turned it on and gasped at the whispy figure in front of me. It looked like a man in a torn 1800s outfit floating above the ground and whispered in a rough voice to me, "You have discovered our treasure," he pointed to me then continued, "congratulations you now get to rot in this cave with us." He gestured to other ghosts. The dean was right about after a challenge there's always another. Now I guess my next one is to make a deal with these spirits to let me go. ☆

Showing Conflicting Feelings in a Personal Narrative

What Writers Do — Writers sometimes create personal narratives that reveal their own mixed feelings about a situation.

What This Writer Does — In this touching personal narrative, Madeline conveys a complex mixture of feelings about her grandmother moving in, adding depth and honesty to her piece.

Activity for your class:

1. Read Madeline's piece aloud or ask a student volunteer to read it with expression.

2. Have students or partners read the story again, noticing words and phrases that convey positive feelings and negative feelings.

3. In the margins, ask them to add + and – signs next to the lines that show positive or negative thoughts or feelings.

4. Share the results as a class and discuss the pattern.

5. Ask students to consider how this pattern impacts them as readers.

Challenge for students:

Look for a piece you have written (or write a new one) in which you explore a mixture of feelings. See if you can lay out a pattern of positive and negative feelings to suit your own narrative or use the text structure below to guide your writing.

Memory Reflection (Mixed Feelings)

Where you were	What happened first and how you felt	What happened next and how you felt differently	What happened last and how you felt	What you thought

A new year tends to spring up on people with surprises of the best and sometimes the worst. We often run into challenges that are hard to get through like walking through molasses as time seems to drag on slowly while life stands still. At the beginning of January, it felt like the year would be a great one with good surprises everywhere I turned. What no one else knew is that I was trying to avoid a challenge I knew would come along. Even before the year started, news came that my Mimi was going to live with us for a whole six months. I love my grandma, but she isn't my favorite person. I knew that with her arrival would come changes my family would have to make in order to have someone else added to our family. My grandma is someone who involves lots of patience because she expects the best, so with the thought of change and her pressuring personality, I feared the day she would show up even with my affection towards her. This challenge was something I was afraid would ruin my year and bring more than enough change.

My dad was gone when I woke up the Saturday before winter break was over. It was a sunny day in which he would usually be outside, but as my mind came into order, I recalled him planning to attend to his wonderful mother-in-law at the airport when the time came. Depression kicked in and made me feel like I was deprived of energy. Weakness would never make me feel better and I knew that. It didn't help much when I was told by my mom to help clean our house before Mimi was there. The only thing I could think was how absurd it was that we had to impress her. Family isn't supposed to care what your house looks like or if it's clean enough. My mom knew she would expect perfection, so she made it that way. It made me so angry to think of how it might be when she actually came. As soon as I was done cleaning, I went to my sacred room

of relaxation to paint pretty pictures and live in the moment.

Even though living in the moment sounded great, I listened hard for when my dad got home. Eventually, I did hear new voices as I cleaned up my paint mess and I knew exactly whose voice it was. The voice was getting closer and when I looked up, the keeper of the voice stood right in front of me. I was almost paralyzed, but I knew I couldn't show it, so I moved into Mimi's embrace and faked my excitement.

That day went incredibly slow just like I imagined the next six months to be. With my grandma there, I felt uncomfortable in my own home, but kept moving on because all you can do in a challenge is keep moving. ☆

Fleshing Out a Kernel Essay With Dialogue

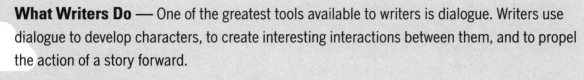

What Writers Do — One of the greatest tools available to writers is dialogue. Writers use dialogue to develop characters, to create interesting interactions between them, and to propel the action of a story forward.

What This Writer Does — Magen skillfully uses dialogue to reveal characters and move her action forward.

Activity for your class:

1. Give students copies of Magen's narrative and read the piece together.

2. Ask students to reread it and to highlight only the dialogue.

3. Then have two students perform these pieces in a choral reading, using only the dialogue.

4. Discuss how the author uses the dialogue to develop her characters, show the relationship between them, and move the action forward.

Challenge for students:

Take one of your kernel essays (or write a new one) and build a narrative by adding dialogue between your characters. Try to use the dialogue to show the reader what your characters are like and how they relate to each other.

Memory Reflection

Where you were	What happened first	What happened next	What happened last	What you thought

It was bright and sunny outside and you could hear the birds chirping and the waves of the swimming pool clashing together in a big boom. It was summer break and me and my cousins were at my Meemaw's house playing in the pool.

"Tori! I bet you five smackaroons that I can run, jump on the trampoline, bounce off, then jump on top of the roof, and swallow ten worms in two minutes...without puking!" I challenged her. Tori was my fifteen year old cousin and practically my best friend. "Sounds like a deal!" she shrilled. "This should be good, considering I'm always right." I mumbled.

Meanwhile, during my preparation for the upcoming event, Tori sat on a bench, waiting and giving me a lot of "what if's?" For example: What if you didn't make it and you fell on the ground and broke your arm? What if you did puke after eating the worms?" "I won't, due to me always being correct." I bragged. "You sure are confident." she notified.

After our conversation we went to the starting line and I was ready to go. "Okay. When I say go you may begin. I will start the clock for two minutes starting...NOW!!" I took off jetting towards the trampoline. It had rained the night before and everything was wet, therefore everything was double the difficulty level. I leaped onto the trampoline and attempted to bounce on top of the roof. "Shoot!" I muttered. I got back on the trampoline and gave it three heavy bounces. I soared through the air like a bald eagle. I landed on the roof with a big thud. "Ouch! Dang that hurt!" I complained. I hopped up after my big fall and took off, pouncing off the roof like a lion during feeding time. I grabbed a shovel and started flinging dirt everywhere. I saw two worms so I yanked them out and swallowed them with no problem. Seven worms later. "I need one more. Come on! There one is!! I screamed to myself. "GULP!" I heard my throat as I swallowed the slimey creature. "5-4-3" Tori was counting down. I sprinted back down the hard, concrete sidewalk. "2-1!" I had barely made it. "Hahaha! In your face! I win! Where's my money? I told you I was right!"

Tori got the money and sadly laid it in my hand. "Woohoo! That was awesome!" I cheered. I was so excited that I had put my mind to something and achieved it. I really was right after all. I guess in the end, being confident really does make a big difference. "Dang! I need some water! Worms have a terrible, horrible after-taste!!" ☆

Showing How a Character Makes an Important Decision

What Writers Do — Writers show what powerful yet conflicting urges we have in life, especially when we are facing difficult choices.

What This Writer Does — Mason creates a mouse narrator who has to make a tough decision, revealing the how the mouse thinks through his decision and considers the possible outcomes of his choice.

Activity for your class:

1. Ask an animated volunteer to read the piece aloud as students follow along on their copies.

2. Have students use highlighters and color-code the piece:
   - green—words or phrases that show the narrator may decide to eat the cheese
   - red—words or phrases that show the narrator may decide to leave the cheese alone

3. Ask students to share their findings. How does the writer reveal the mouse's powerful drives to both eat and resist the cheese?

Challenge for students:

Write about a decision you have faced. Color-code each side of the decision in your piece. Have you shown the reader the struggle you experienced making a choice?

A Completely Made-Up Story

Characters doing something	Problem arises	How they try to solve it	How they solve it

The house was very dark and vacant as I lay my eyes upon it. Carefully, I crawled across the street, up to the front door. No lights were on inside the house, and all the doors were shut and locked. Luckily, I was able to stumble upon a doggie-door in the backyard. I stared down the opening, then sprinted toward it.

I had made it into the house! My stomach was grumbling, and I felt a pain on my side. My withered body needed food badly.

The house was nicely decorated, with colorful furniture, velvet drapes, granite counter-tops, flat-panel TV's, but no food to be found. I walked through the house, quiet as a mouse, you could say. It seemed that the walls were closing in on me, as I stumbled through long, narrow hallways. I was searching the house head to toe, but couldn't find any EDIBLE substances.

As I neared the corner of a bedroom, I witnessed a helpless piece of sharp cheddar cheese. My mouth was drooling now. Slyly, I inched towards my dinner, hoping not to be spotted by a human.

Once I was in reaching distance of the cheese, I noticed something connected with my food. It was a series of tiny metal bars, all attached to the piece of cheese. My food was placed on a platform, and it almost looked like if I lifted the cheese, a bar would click and smash me. This discovery really made me ponder about the price I'd have to pay to get food. I gazed upon the delicious cheese, then the trap. The cheese was so tempting, but the trap might kill me. My mind was going haywire, yes or no, I couldn't decide. Sweat was dripping down my face, through the hairs on my body, and into the soft, fluffy carpet.

Finally, I had made my decision. I ran through the dining room, across the kitchen, and out the doggie-door. I feel that risking your life for food is not worth the outcome. This time I was truly RIGHT. Sometimes in life acting on impulse is a really bad move. ☆

Choosing Vivid Verbs

What Writers Do — Writers choose precise, vivid verbs that paint a picture in their readers' minds.

What This Writer Does — In this fictional narrative, Raymond's use of vivid verbs is masterful, filling his story with intensity and imagery for the reader.

Activity for your class:

1. Pass out copies of the piece.

2. Ask a student to read the piece aloud while the class follows along on their copies.

3. Place students in small groups and have them read through it again, highlighting some of the crisp, well-chosen verbs.

4. Ask them to replace some of these vivid verbs with more bland choices (for example, *"A woman walked through the market"* instead of *"scampered briskly"*).

5. Ask students to share some of these new sentences with the class. Discuss the contrast.

6. Make a wall chart of vivid verbs and add to it throughout the year.

Challenge for students:

On an index card, write a paragraph about arriving someplace (like your local grocery store) and walking inside. Try using vivid verbs and seeing how many interesting details you can add to an ordinary scene, the way Raymond did.

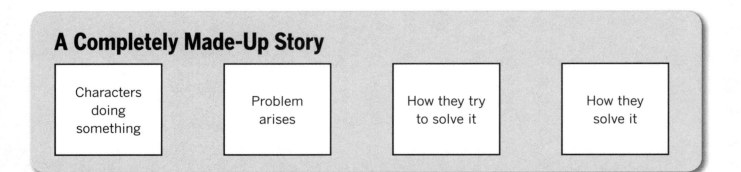

A Completely Made-Up Story

| Characters doing something | Problem arises | How they try to solve it | How they solve it |

A Gift Worth Giving

A woman scampered briskly through the local market. Merchants yelled at pedestrians to purchace their wares. At the market, anything could be bought or sold. The woman payed little attention to the merchants. Instead she scanned the throng of people before her for her son, young William. Young William had disappeared while his mother was doing business. Frantically, she searched and searched for young William, but he was nowhere to be found.

William traipsed along the stalls of merchants, looking for something to buy. He wished he could find something to spend his money on. William loved to spend money. Even when he had none, he always wished he did. Today especially though, he wanted to spend his money on something special for his mother. Her birthday was soon, and he wanted to give her something she would remember forever. William had snuck out from behind his mother while she had been browsing the oceanic wares of a sea merchant. William had thought that sneaking away would not alarm his mother, but he was dead wrong. His mother would be very mad at him. His mother was not mad very often. She was lucky to even have William. William browsed more merchants, intent on his goal. Sure enough, he finally found something she would love. He had found an old wooden box that could be used to store jewlrey. On the rectangular lid, a mural of a tiger stalking its prey was presented. William's mother, who loved tigers, would like this a lot. Now that he had found the perfect gift for his mother, he skipped back to where he had left her. The only problem was, she was not there. William now knew that wandering off without her had not been such a good idea.

"Mother!" William yelled in vain, "Mother!" His mother was gone, and he was alone. Alone in a hostile and untrustworthy world. Then, Nico, his good friend, grabbed him and escorted him through the throng and to his mother. "Thanks Nic!" William screamed with joy. Nico just smiled. William's mother embraced him as if he had been away for weeks. "I just wanted to surprise you," William explained as he handed his mother the box. As soon as she set eyes on it, she was in love. William was right, she did love it. ☆

Writing Dialogue With Inner Reactions

What Writers Do — Writers weave spoken dialogue with their unspoken reactions, giving readers a rare glimpse at what goes on *inside* a person's head.

What This Writer Does — Sarah narrates her mental reactions to the words spoken around her, revealing to readers her insight, thoughts, and feelings.

Activity for your class:

1. Pass out copies and read Sarah's personal narrative together with your class.

2. Have students highlight all of Sarah's mental reactions during her experience at the spelling bee.

3. Then read the piece aloud *without* the highlighted mental reactions. What differences do you notice? Discuss.

Challenge for students:

Select a piece of your own writing. Try adding a pattern of dialogue and reaction, like this:

- You:

- Your friend:

- Your mental reaction or what you thought about what your friend said.

Memory Reflection

Where you were	What happened first	What happened next	What happened last	What you thought

"Your word is caper," she said. "Caper?" I repeated back. The pronouncer nodded patiently but her eyebrows furrowed in evident annoyance at my inability to just spell the word. I swallowed and then licked my lips. I had seen this word before in a book about pirates. I knew how to spell it! Slowly, but deliberately, I began to spell the word: "C-A-P-E-R, caper," I said. I didn't look toward the judge's table because I couldn't bear to see one of them reach over and pick up that little brass bell which, if rung, would indicate that I was out. But I did not hear the little brass bell ring, so I listened instead for those three magic words, the ones that, if said, meant I still had a chance...then I heard "That is correct."

I sat patiently in my chair as I looked around and saw many people in the stands talking amongst themselves in hushed voices. I leaned slightly to my right and whispered into my friend's ear, "I'm nervous." "Why?" she asked, "I mean, you are the best speller in the class." It was true that I always made 100's on my spelling tests, but this was different. You didn't get to study the words in advance.

"Okay, ladies and gentlemen, if you'd please take your seats, we're about ready to begin the spelling bee," said the pronouncer. My stomach lurched at those words, and I felt like I might hurl; it was with that feeling that the spelling bee began. The words in the first few rounds were fairly easy, though some people got out. My friend, Bridgette, and I were still in, that is, until the fourth round. Bridgette walked up to the microphone, but she spelled her word too fast and missed a letter. The judges rang a little brass bell and Bridgette was out. I managed to stay in for the next two rounds by correctly spelling "caper" and "disengage." Now only this short, blonde haired boy and I were left. The boy stepped up to the microphone haughtily and with great confidence. He made me feel anxious just sitting there. The boy's word was "relevant," but he spelled it R-E-L-E-V-E-N-T. The brass bell rang and the boy sat down. I knew even if I spelled "relevant" right, I'd have to spell another word correctly to win. I stood up and walked to the microphone as the pronouncer gave me the word again. I spelled it correctly and the butterflies in my stomach felt more excited than nervous. The pronouncer gave me my next word: "Endeavor," she said. The word was somewhat familiar, but I couldn't think of where I'd seen it before. My time was limited, so I gave it my best shot. "E-N-D-E-A-V-O-R," I said. I held my breath and strained my ears, and all I heard was three words...

I did win my school spelling bee and I went on to county where I placed second. I've never gone further than that in any other spelling bee before or after that time, but spelling remains, to this day, to be something I'm really good at, something I've learned that I do well. ☆

Using Time Transitions: Flash Forward

What Writers Do — Writers rarely retell events in actual time. Instead, they move from the present to a flashback (a moment in the past) or jump ahead, moving from one important moment to another.

What This Writer Does — Soo masterfully handles the passage of time by zooming from one important moment to another. This choice moves the action forward swiftly, creating a quick pace and engaging read.

Activity for your class:

1. Read the piece with the class and find the place where the writer moves from "Scene One" to "Scene Two." (*It was Saturday.*)

2. Have students highlight the sentences that tell the reader that an amount of time has passed (for example, *The day had finally arrived. I arrived at the community center...*)

3. Discuss what events the writer skipped over and why she might have made this decision.

Challenge for students:

Find a piece that you have written (or write a new one) and find a place to flash forward, using Soo's pattern. See if you can find other places where it would improve the piece to jump ahead in time.

Memory Reflection

Where you were	What happened first	What happened next	What happened last	What you thought

The Spicy Seafood Secret Disaster

"Help is needed in aisle four. Thank you." The loud intercom announced. Looking around, I asked, "So do you want to tell us why you brought us here?" My friend, Sasha, brought me and another friend, Lilly, to Wal-Mart, and we had no clue why. "Look over there." Sasha replied, pointing at a box in the front of the large store. "What about it?" Lilly asked. "It's not just an ordinary box. It's the box that holds the key to my future." she replied. Lilly and I stared at her very confused. "That is Rachel Ray's Teen Cook-off auditions box. Only ten groups can sign up and I have one of the entry forms," she explained. We stared at her again, even more confused. Looking annoyed, she said, "I'm going to enter this contest. If you're one of the two final groups, you get to meet Rachel Ray. You know she's my hero and I just have to meet her. And if you're the winning group, you receive a full scholarship to the world's most finest culinary arts school! Do you follow?" We nodded our heads. "Ok. But to enter you have to be in a group of three or more. So I entered you guys as my group," she announced. Our jaws dropped. Sasha was a good cook, but us? With that being announced, she went over to the box and dropped the entry form into the slot.

"Why? You didn't even ask us if we wanted to be in your group. I don't want to," I whined. "Chill it, Stace. All you have to do is memorize the recipe, and call it out to us on the day of the audition. See? It's easy work." Sasha tried to comfort me. "Ok. But I'm only doing this because you're my friend." I gave in. "Thank you! You're the best!" she squealed and gave me a hug. "So, what are we making?" Lilly asked. "My Granny's Famous Spicy Seafood Secret, my version," she replied. Lilly was horrified. Before she could say a word though, Sasha continued on, "Don't worry Lilly. My Granny gave me the recipe and I worked on it several times. The recipe is very easy to make." "Someone tell me why Lilly looks like she just saw a ghost." I demanded. "She saw my Granny make this dish, and she knows it's very complicated to make. That's why." Sasha explained,

"But since it's my version, it'll be better for you to memorize. But you have to get everything right. If one measurement is wrong, we'll be disqualified. OK?" She handed me the neatly-written recipe. "I'll see you at the Community Center on Saturday at nine. Bye!" "This is going to be a piece of pie," I thought. This was where I was first wrong.

It was Saturday. The day had finally arrived. I was ready. I knew that recipe like it was an everyday thing. I arrived at the Community Center and checked in. I hurried over to my station where Sasha and Lilly were. "Beep!" a whistle blew. "Let's go get our ingredients!" Lilly yelled. "Shrimp. Crab. Oysters. Squid…," I called out the ingredients one by one from the top of my head. When we had everything I started to list the preparation steps. "Devain the shrimp. Cut the squid and octopus into an edible size."

All the preparations were done and we only needed to make the spicy sauce while the seafood part was cooking. "Ok. Mix two tablespoons of vinegar with hm…" I couldn't remember how many tablespoons of the chili powder to put in! And this being spicy, the chili powder was very important to this recipe. Then the number five and a half popped into my mind. "What a relief!" I thought, "if I hadn't remembered, that would've been horrible. "Ok, we're done!" Sasha exclamed. She handed the judges our food and stepped back. "Hey, Stacey, are you sure it's five and a half tablespoon?" she asked. "Yes, I'm sure. Don't worry. We got this." I assured her. Just then the judges turned beet red and were screaming for water. They had eaten our food. "Sasha, it was suppose to be five and a half teaspoons." I told her, "I'm sorry." She realized it was our food that was making the judges dance. "It's ok. I should've checked before we turned it in. There's always next year." We stood there and laughed at the sight of the judges screaming for water. ☆

Using Absolutes as Sentence Fragments

What Writers Do — Writers sometimes create vivid images in a concise form by using a quick succession of sentence fragments.

What This Writer Does — Stefan uses a series of descriptive sentence fragments together with a second-person point of view to plunge the reader, physically, into his shoes. This creates an exciting and intriguing lead.

Activity for your class:

1. Pass out copies of the piece.

2. Read the first paragraph aloud as students follow along on their copies.

3. Explain that writers sometimes use sentence fragments deliberately for effect.

4. Read Stefan's introductory paragraph again and ask students to highlight the absolutes as they hear them. (for example, *motor ringing, vibrations shaking*)

5. Compare it to a more ordinary lead, like, *"Have you ever ridden a dirt bike? I have."* Discuss.

Challenge for students:

Find a piece of your own writing with lots of action. Try to imitate Stefan's lead by writing a second-person barrage of sensory sentence fragments for your piece. To surprise your reader, you might also want to conceal the topic of your piece until the very end of the opening—the way Stefan did.

Memory Reflection

Where you were	What happened first	What happened next	What happened last	What you thought

Vroom! The sound of the powerful motor ringing in your ears, the vibrations shaking your body. The wind pounding in every inch of your aching body. Rays of sun blinding you, through leaves of towering trees. The weight of thick plastic covering most of your sweat drenched, thick polyester uniform. Your muscles aching from the constant jerking of a hundred and fifty pound beast. The exhaustion from the endless hours and every minute seeming as it were an hour. Your eyes peeled open for the unexpected, your mind dreading to blink, the dryness of your eyes causing a dreadful burning sensation throughout your face. Your heart beating from the adrenaline of swerving through a tedious path of rocks and dirty sand, sticks, nearly being decapitated by low hanging branches of solid trees. Focusing on avoiding the slightest mistake, for it could be the result of a great deal of pain or perhaps death. The fear of the unknown that lies ahead. This for me this is a typical yet still amazing weekend riding my dirt bike.

This wonderful, incredible, unforgettable experience is the result of five years of strong determination and many challenging defeats of hurdles thrown towards myself, as I learned to master the sport of dirt bike racing. Five years previous to now, the thought of riding a dirt bike never occurred to me. Even though I admired almost everybody who had ever touched a dirt bike, I hadn't dreamed of riding one. However my thoughts on the subject were endless.

My step dad had introduced me to dirt bikes. He was a skilled and experienced rider. Whenever my parents had seen the way dirt bikes inspired me, they worked to make my dream of riding come true. When they first told me this I was both nervous and excited. I felt like there was a zoo in my stomach, no words could compare to the joy in my heart.

When I first started to learn, I was clueless. I would fall left and right. Even though I was constantly sore I practiced, as much as possible. The famous words, "Practice makes perfect" were constantly lingering through my head. Gradually I got better and better. My mind was focused on speed and oblivious to the possible consequences of my actions.

After about two years of raising the bar to heights of skill level I never thought possible, I came to a big bump in the road. I had damaged my bike beyond repair, and to top that my parents were having a divorce. Only races away from the great pride of being a youth pro, it was over. My mom and I had to move and start over from scratch, no car, no house, no money.

Over the time of a couple of months, my future in dirt bikes had turned from the dark of night, to the light of day. My mother made the ultimate commitment and bought both of us new bikes. Even though I had lost much skill, my dream to make it to the top was reborn, bigger, faster, and better than I ever thought possible. I shall continue my adventure to the top, nearly a youth pro. ☆

Using Time Transitions: Flashbacks

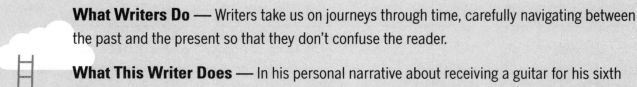

What Writers Do — Writers take us on journeys through time, carefully navigating between the past and the present so that they don't confuse the reader.

What This Writer Does — In his personal narrative about receiving a guitar for his sixth birthday, Taylor manages time shifts well, flawlessly moving from present to past, then back to present.

Activity for your class:

1. Distribute copies of Taylor's story and have students read the piece with a partner.

2. Ask them to highlight the words and phrases that show a time shift. (for example, *"It was my 6th birthday…" "…seven years later…"*)

3. Have students look for the following:

   - Taylor's organizational pattern (he has a memory from the past—a flashback—framed on either side by the present).

   - Where he changed verb tenses (for example, from *I am* to the past tense *I was* when he flashes back).

4. Ask, why did he change tenses? (*to indicate a flashback*).

Challenge for students:

Write a personal narrative about getting something special when you were younger. Try organizing your piece around a time shift, like Taylor did. Don't forget to show the reader how this experience changed your life.

Memory Reflection

Where you were	What happened first	What happened next	What happened last	What you thought

We all want to be rockstars, right? We all want to be rich, famous and really popular. Right?! Well I sure do! By the time I'm 20, I want everyone to know who I am. But, it isn't as easy as it looks to become famous. It's hard work! You have to build your way to the top. I don't want to brag or anything, but I'm a pretty good guitar player. But, I haven't always been this good. When I got my first guitar, I couldn't play half the things I can play now! We all have to start somewhere…

It was my 6th birthday and I was spending it with my great-grandparents. "Woohoo!" I thought as I ripped one present open after another. I had a pile of wrapping paper to my left, and a pile of presents to my right. I guess you can say I was spoiled. I loved the sound wrapping paper made when I ripped it off a present! RRRIIIPPP!!! It reminded me of lightning crashing in a thunderstorm! As I grabbed my last present from my grandmother, I noticed its funny shape. It looked kind of like a long deformed rock and it felt like it too. But, I didn't care. I just wanted to hear the incredible rip from the tearing of the wrapping paper!

I ripped the wrapping paper off the present, but didn't hear the familiar ripping sound. Instead, I heard a jumble of musical notes! It was a guitar! I held up my guitar for my grandparents to see, and they smiled at me like it was the proudest moment of their lives. I positioned the guitar in my lap, and slowly strummed the guitar. As I heard the strings harmonize, I let out a joyous laugh. Why, you ask? Because, on that day, I truly felt like a rockstar!

Now, seven years later, I am an awesome guitar player. I've even written my own music! Everyday, since I acquired my first guitar, I've been practicing. Practice makes perfect. Even though I've gotten new and better guitars over the years, I still have my first guitar. I keep it so I'll never forget how much you can improve if you put your mind and strength into it. It doesn't matter who you are, or what you do for a living. There's a rockstar inside of everybody. ☆

Withholding and Revealing Information to Build Suspense

What Writers Do — Writers make choices about how much information they are going to give to readers and when. Withholding key information until just the right moment can build suspense. This withholding-and-revealing skill is a powerful tool for writers.

What This Writer Does — In this excellent fictional account of a historical event, Tyler weaves in a web of clues about his story's setting. It is not until the end that he reveals the one detail that confirms what his reader suspects.

Activity for your class:

1. Hand out copies of the piece.

2. Read the piece aloud as students follow along.

3. Independently or in pairs, have students highlight words and phrases in the selection that answer these questions:
   - Did you suspect where the story was set? When did you suspect it?
   - What clues did you notice about the time period?
   - When were you sure about the setting?

4. In a large group, compare what the students highlighted and discuss how the use of clues builds the suspense.

Challenge for students:

Create a fictional narrator and write a first-person account about a moment in history. Be sure to include factual details. You may want to withhold a defining piece of information until the end, like Tyler did.

Memory Reflection

Where you were	What happened first	What happened next	What happened last	What you thought

History's Ship

I gazed at the tickets I had purchased two days ago in awe, as this would be my final hour with them. Today, I would be migrating to America on what is sure to be the ship of the century! A gargantuan cruiser from the White Star Line. I was waiting at the docks as the crowd burst into a frenzy. The majestic ship had just arrived, and the boarding ramp was open. Everyone charged on board, eager to explore this historical first.

The first thing I did when I got to my cabin was sleep. I had been so jittery with the news that I would buy tickets, I hadn't slept since then. After preparing myself for the day, I went on an expedition through the giant cruiser, and this solidified my belief that this would be a sea crossing to remember forever. At every turn, I discovered a new room and luxury, and I trekked through the ship until I arrived at the second-class lounge, which was fit for a king. Paintings hung on the walls, and exotic designs dotted the room. The first aspect I noticed was the card table with men laughing merrily all around. I quickly joined their group, and I was addicted within minutes. For hours we played poker and blackjack, only stopping to eat, a jolly mood filling the areas.

What snapped me out of my jovial trance was an earsplitting scraping sound, and everyone was thrown into a panic. After awhile, some of us forgot about it and continued our games of merriment, while others headed upstairs to investigate. Soon my anxiety got the best of me. As I reached the top deck, I realized there was nothing wrong. The ship had just smashed an iceberg, with pieces of it flying on deck. This would surely be one for the history books! Not only is this the largest ship ever built, but it just wrecked an iceberg! Even the names of the passengers may be remembered forever!

My mind changed suddenly. Third-class passengers stormed the upper deck, and the crew prepared lifeboats. What was going on? That was when it dawned on everyone, as well as myself. We were sinking. Passengers scurried to the lifeboats, and I snuck aboard one of last lifeboats to depart. As we drifted into the sea, I knew we would go down in history in a different way than I expected. I threw one last glance at the doomed cruiser. I spotted the Titanic's name fall just underneath the water line. ☆

Using Anadiplosis to Make a Truism Chain

What Writers Do — Writers use rhetorical devices to capture their listener's ear, stir emotions, or emphasize a point. *Anadiplosis* (an-uh-duh-PLOH-sus)—the repetition of the last word or phrase from the previous sentence at the beginning of the next—is one such device.

What This Writer Does — Zachary uses anadiplosis beautifully in his conclusion, creating an effective and memorable "chain" of thoughts and ideas that will linger in the minds of readers and stir their emotions.

Activity for your class:

1. Distribute copies of the piece and read it together.

2. Reread the first sentence, asking students to circle the repeated words (*hard work*).

3. Next, have them draw lines connecting the repeated words. Look at the chain that this creates.

4. Identify the author's dream (...*play for the University of Texas...go to the pros...become a Hall of Fame legend*).

5. Explain the term *anadiplosis*. As a class, find and label the double anadiplosis in the last paragraph. Talk about how the use of anadiplosis gives power to the writer's discussion of what it will take to achieve his dream. Notice the truism train.

Challenge for students:

Write about a dream you have. Try using the text structure below and creating anadiplosis "chains" to stir your readers' emotions.

Anadiplosis

Truism chain	My dream (why I had it)	How I started to achieve the dream	How I finally reached the dream	Truism chain

Dedication: it leads to hard work and hard work teaches you to do something well. And that's pretty much where my story begins. With dedication and hard work.

It all started ever since I was little. My dad would take me to a park to work on my skills, daily. Whether it was just learning to field a ground ball or learning to crow-hop to easily throw out a runner from the outfield, he taught me how to. I remember going out to the fields and every time I smelt that elegant smell of the outfield grass, or felt the rocks and the dirt from the infield slide across my body as I dove for another ball thinking, "Good job. Way to give it your all!" I love that. For some reason I love the pain of the rocks. Some people hate it, but to me, it's like a high dollar massage. And for me, I'd rather be in a hundred degree weather working my rear off than in some water park, any day. That's because I have a dream. I dream that I will go to the University of Texas in Austin to play baseball for the Longhorns on a full scholarship. Then, I will go to the pros and become a Hall of Fame baseball legend. That's my dream and I'm willing to do anything to reach my dream. I practice as much as I can to be a better athlete.

A few years ago while I was in Little League it was spring break and we had one more game, plus if you had made the All Stars, you would have that. And as spring break came my parents were talking about where we wanted to go. And when they asked me I said, "Nowhere, I want to stay here and practice so I can make All Stars." So while everyone else was on vacation, I was at the fields practicing my heart out. I would stay there and learn how to do all kinds of things that I never even knew existed. I learned to drop step, back hand, forehand, and all kinds of stuff. And when spring break was over and we had our game, I amazed everyone there with my fielding. The next week or so I was in my room and my dad called me and said, "Zach, guess what? You made All Stars!" I was so happy. My dad also told me that they said my fielding was amazing! It felt so good to know that somebody else thought that you learned how to field better than anyone else.

Practicing hard means giving it your all. Giving it your all helps you master that skill. And mastering those skills means you achieve your dreams. ☆

Using Enumeratio to Add Detail

What Writers Do — Writers use a rhetorical device called *enumeratio*—or *enumeration*—in their writing to provide their readers with lists of key details. These lists create images, set moods, and serve to amplify and intensify a piece of text.

What This Writer Does — Keri uses enumeratio, masterfully crafting lists into her sentences to paint clear images for the reader. In this way, she packs a lot of detail into a small space.

Activity for your class:

1. Pass out copies of Keri's piece and read it out loud.

2. Together with the class, look at this sentence:

    "She washed my uniform nightly, took me to all my classes, coached me when I fought, helped me practice at home and always reminded me to brush my teeth before class."

    Ask: What makes this sentence powerful? (*the list of specifics*)

3. Explain to students that Keri is using a rhetorical device called enumeratio (e-nu-me-RA-tio), listing or detailing the parts of something to amplify or make a point.

4. Ask students to rewrite that sentence, changing the specifics to a generalization. (Example: "*She did so many things*") What is the difference in the impact of the sentence?

5. Have students look at the last sentence of Keri's piece and rewrite it in the same way. Compare the sentences. Discuss students' responses to them.

Challenge for students:

Choose a piece of writing that you are working on. Take one or two of your own sentences and see if you can use enumeratio to break it out into a list of specifics.

Memory Reflection

Where you were	What happened first	What happened next	What happened last	What you thought

"Yeah, but she's a nerd."

As a young girl I wasn't your popular, athletic, brunette goddess. I was the blonde-haired girl who always got straight "A"s and made friends with all the teachers. I wore my school uniform and couldn't shoot a basketball into the hoop even if my life depended on it. When I finally did find a sport that captured my interest, there wasn't a team for my age group that I could join. Therefore, my mom enrolled me in a month's worth of Tae Kwon Do classes.

I instantly fell in love with the sport. My addiction to doing better drove me to become a member of the Jr. Olympic team. I medaled at all my tournaments; I'm the most proud of getting second place at Nationals for Jr. Olympics. Many people questioned why I never gave up. By taking a look at my planner you could tell how devoted I was: five or six days a week I was at the studio practicing.

My alarm sounded off, "Beep. Beep. Beep," and I rolled over, very sore from the previous day's work out. "5:30 a.m., right on time," I would say every Sunday morning as I pressed the snooze button. When I finally forced myself out of bed, I got dressed and went to practice. "There are three thirds to winning: you, your coach, and your support team. If you're missing any of those, there is absolutely no way you can walk or limp out of a ring with a gold medal around your neck," Coach Levell said to us every weekend.

After 8th grade we moved from California to Texas. I had to start from ground zero. Everything was new and I had no friends. I started Tae Kwon Do at a new studio. This was supposed to be the year I tested for my black belt, a goal I had had for four years. However, I wasn't nearly as motivated or dedicated. I skipped practices, my endurance slowly began to weaken and I became more active in other things.

But encouragement isn't only about physically rooting someone on; it's also about knowing someone deep down and helping them in any way so that they get to where they need to be. My lack of enthusiasm did not go unnoticed; my mom was right there. My mom was my savior, my provider, my best friend and my number one cheerleader. She knew how badly I've always wanted my black belt and she encouraged me to get it. She washed my uniform nightly, took me to all my classes, coached me when I fought, helped me practice at home and always reminded me to brush my teeth before class. When there was no one left for me to turn to, my mom was already standing there and helping me get back up and kicking again.

When the test finally came and I waited to be called up to perform, I got nervous. I had sweaty palms, a panicking quickness in my breath and I only heard, "Stop now, you can't do it," thundering to the pulsating roar in my head. The only thing that kept my focus was knowing that someone who believed in me was back there cheering and mentally chanting, "Impossible and can't are not words in our dictionary." After seven hours had passed, I walked out of the studio as a black belt. I had "passed with flying colors." But people don't win in Tae Kwon Do out of sheer luck, the gold medalists are the ones with the most skill and the best support team.

In my life my mom played many roles, but none compare to her role as my #1 cheerleader. Encouragement from others is like a crutch from the heart to aid someone in desperation. Because of my crutch, I'm a black belt, a junior Olympian, a straight "A" student, and a very thankful human. ☆

Layering Thinking and Dialogue

What Writers Do — Writers use many different techniques to allow a reader to see through their eyes. One of these involves revealing the narrator's silent thoughts or reactions.

What This Writer Does — Cassie puts her father's words into dialogue, in direct quotes. She follows his words with her silent reactions.

Activity for your class:

1. Pass out copies of Cassie's piece and read it together with the class.

2. First, ask students to highlight the words her father said using one color.

3. Next, have them highlight Cassie's mental reactions or thoughts using a different color.

4. Ask: What do you see? How would it impact the story if you took her reactions away?

Challenge for students:

Find a piece of writing in your journal or portfolio in which you are the narrator and you are talking with another person. Write the conversation in dialogue using direct quotes. After the other person's words, include some of your own mental reactions.

Memory Reflection

Where you were	What happened first	What happened next	What happened last	What you thought

"Cassie, we need to talk," said my father in a low and suspicious voice. The tone revealed something important, somehow, I knew we were starting a long, monumental discussion.

"Ok, what about," I replied tentatively.

"About, about wills," he stumbled. "I feel now is a good time for you to decide. You are mature enough, and strong enough to make this decision." I think he was more stressed than I was, and he was not even making the choice. "First," he said as he cleared his throat, "we have to talk about Lindsey."

"Um, what do we have to say, we already know she is going to live with you," I announced.

"Yes, but that is what these wills are about, to understand and make clear exactly what happens to her after I'm gone," he said, fading out in the last few words.

"Well, don't plan on dying soon, and maybe by then, who knows, maybe she can support herself."

"Cassie, think of who you are talking about. It's Lindsey. I've told you she will never grow out of her ADD, an extreme learning disability, and even if she could live with it, her social skills just don't function like the rest of the world. She functions on a 5th grade level. She's a ten year old, stuck in a twenty year old body." Wow. It really hit me then, my sister, my lovely twenty-year-old sister will probably never function as a "normal" human being. Someone will always have to at least check up on her or permanently live with her. I took a moment then strongly looked into my father's deep blue eyes. I could see his struggle and fear. Lindsey was his little baby girl and he couldn't and wouldn't let anything happen to her.

"What are my options?" I forcefully asked.

"Great!" he gave a sigh of relief. "There's the possibility of her living with you, putting her in a group home, or finding a foster care situation," he exclaimed, putting a huge emphasis on "living with you." "Now you don't have to decide now, take your time and think it through." I didn't have a clue. I could go all different directions and had so many reasons, but I still ended up with her living with me. It was just the best situation for her, so there was no way around it.

"I want her to live with me." The words just popped out of my mouth. I was confident, but a little startled.

"What? You have decided already? You should take more time," he said, stunned that I replied so quickly.

"No, no, I've decided and I choose to take full responsibility of Lindsey after you are gone."

"You're sure? There's no turning back," he said. "Then sign here and I'll take care of the rest of it. Thank you sweety, you made the right choice."

"Thank you, Daddy," I beamed as I gave him a huge hug.

That night, as I was lying in bed, I realized how an important choice such as signing a will can impact someone's life. For Lindsey, her life will continue, happy as expected, but another choice might not conclude that way. So you have to stop and ask yourself, "How does my choice affect and possibly change someone's life?" ☆

Using Transitions to Develop a Conclusion

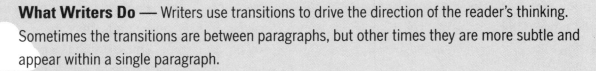

What Writers Do — Writers use transitions to drive the direction of the reader's thinking. Sometimes the transitions are between paragraphs, but other times they are more subtle and appear within a single paragraph.

What This Writer Does — Elisa's last paragraph is a stunning example of sentence-to-sentence progression using transitional words and phrases.

Activity for your class:

1. Give each student an index card. Ask students to choose a person to write about and place that person's name at the top of the card.

2. Next, have them write a sentence about that person that includes one characteristic, using this pattern: "_____ was _____." (for example, "*My grandmother was kind.*" Or "*My brother was stingy.*")

3. Ask students to then write a new sentence about one thing they saw that person do that demonstrates that characteristic.

   Next, have them complete a third sentence using this sentence stem:

   "*When asked why he (or she) behaved in this manner, _____.*"

4. Write a next sentence beginning with, "*Gradually...*"

5. Have them write the last sentence beginning with, "*To this day...*"

6. Share the paragraphs aloud.

7. Now read Elisa's narrative to the class. Together, look at Elisa's last paragraph and compare it to the student samples. Discuss the effectiveness of her conclusion.

Challenge for students:

Try using this pattern, or a similar pattern you create, as the conclusion to a fictional narrative like Elisa's or for an expository piece about a person you admire.

A Completely Made-Up Story

Where you were	What happened first	What happened next	What happened last	What you thought

Once, in a bog not far from here, there lived a toad. Timothy Toad, they called him, and he was a very nice toad, though not very pretty. His skin was all brown and warty, and his eyes were yellow and watery. However, despite his appearance, Timothy had many friends.

One day as he was hopping along merrily, Timothy saw a sight that bewitched him. He had laid eyes on a fairy. Not just any fairy, but the Great Fairy of the Bog, other wise known as Magenta. Timothy instantly fell in love with the Great Fairy. He admired her pearly, glossy wings and lusted after the deep violet hue that radiated from the pixie's fair skin. Her chestnut hair and light blue eyes beckoned to Timothy and forgetting who and what he was, he stepped forth into the clearing.

Magenta, a beautiful yet narcissistic sprite, took one look at Timothy and nearly flew away. "What business have you here, toad?" Magenta asked naughtily.

"None, except my wish to look upon your grace, for I believe that I am in love," answered Timothy courteously.

"Love? Thou believest that one as lovely as I would take interest in thee? Ha! Surely you jest, O Squatting One," Magenta replied most disrespectfully. She took notice of the many warts that plagued his brown patchy skin. She became repulsed at the sight of those watery, yellow eyes that looked in admiration at her. "Oh, what funny legs!" She thought to herself, "Surely, I, Magenta, the Great Fairy of the Bog deserve better than this beast?"

"Be gone!" she said finally, after a long pause of silence. "I have no time to sit here and waste my time with one so unworthy as you." And with a flick of glittery wings, she left the poor toad weeping in the clearing.

Timothy was heartbroken. He wouldn't eat and wouldn't sleep. He stopped conversing with friends and neighbors and became bitter towards all. When asked why he behaved in this manner, he merely replied, "Blame it on the so called Great Fairy." Gradually, his friends gave up and just left him alone. To this day, he sits alone on his stump and both curses and longs for the Great Fairy, Magenta. ☆

Weaving Together Text From Different Genres

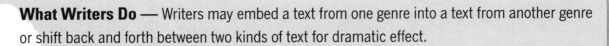

What Writers Do — Writers may embed a text from one genre into a text from another genre or shift back and forth between two kinds of text for dramatic effect.

What This Writer Does — Sherilynn weaves the text of a prayer into her realistic fiction, creating a chilling effect.

Activity for your class:

1. Pass out copies of the piece and have two students read it aloud, with one reading the narrative and one reading the prayer.

2. Discuss with the class how the woven text worked together to impact the reader. What is the effect? Why?

Challenge for students:

Choose a piece of your own writing. See if you can come up with a piece of well-known, recognizable text to weave into it the way Sherilynn did (for example, lyrics to a religious, patriotic, or popular song, a poem, a quote, or something else). You might want to try using the text structure below if it fits your piece.

Downfall

| How bad things are now | Flashback to happier days | Details about how bad things are now | My feelings now |

"Our Father who art in heaven, hallowed be thy name..."

About a year and a half ago my mother and father got involved in drugs and alcohol.

"Thy kingdom come, thy will be done on earth as it is in heaven..."

My mother helplessly lies on the couch watching and hypnotized by the TV after taking in too much crack or weed. My dad...well he is a drunkie!!

"Give us this day our daily bread, and forgive our trespasses, as we forgive those who trespass against us..."

On weekdays I have to get what I need myself, because my parents are completely oblivious to the fact that I was ever born.

"And lead us not into temptation, but deliver us from evil..."

I remember when I was younger that my mom would take me to the park and we would have a picnic. She would make elegant and elaborate meals—not just peanut butter and jelly sandwiches.

"For thy is the kingdom and the power, and glory forever..."

My name is Katelyn Rashea Dickerson, I'm 11 years old and live in a one bedroom apartment. As I told you previously, my mom does drugs and my dad drinks to his hearts content. My father goes out every night and doesn't come home till 2 maybe 3 in the morning. When he does...he is like a bull in a china closet, throwing things and slamming doors and yelling at everything. One night he busted into my room and pulled me to the living room, ran his finger along the entertainment center and said, "Do you see this dust;" even though I had not seen anything. I had dusted it earlier that day. "Y-y-yes sir," I stuttered. "I want it spotless when I get back in here!" he exclaimed. And of course he isn't gone long enough for me to finish, Oh NO!! he hits me till I can barely stand...then it is off to the bathroom. He bangs my head against the mirror and the counter top. After a few grueling minutes of punishment, it is over, he has had his fun for the night. One night he came home in a drunk rage and beat the hell out of me. He stomped off and got a gun. Two shots, one for him and the other for my mom.

Ever since my father turned into a monster I have been afraid of anyone who tries to touch me—even if they are trying to help.

"...Amen" ☆

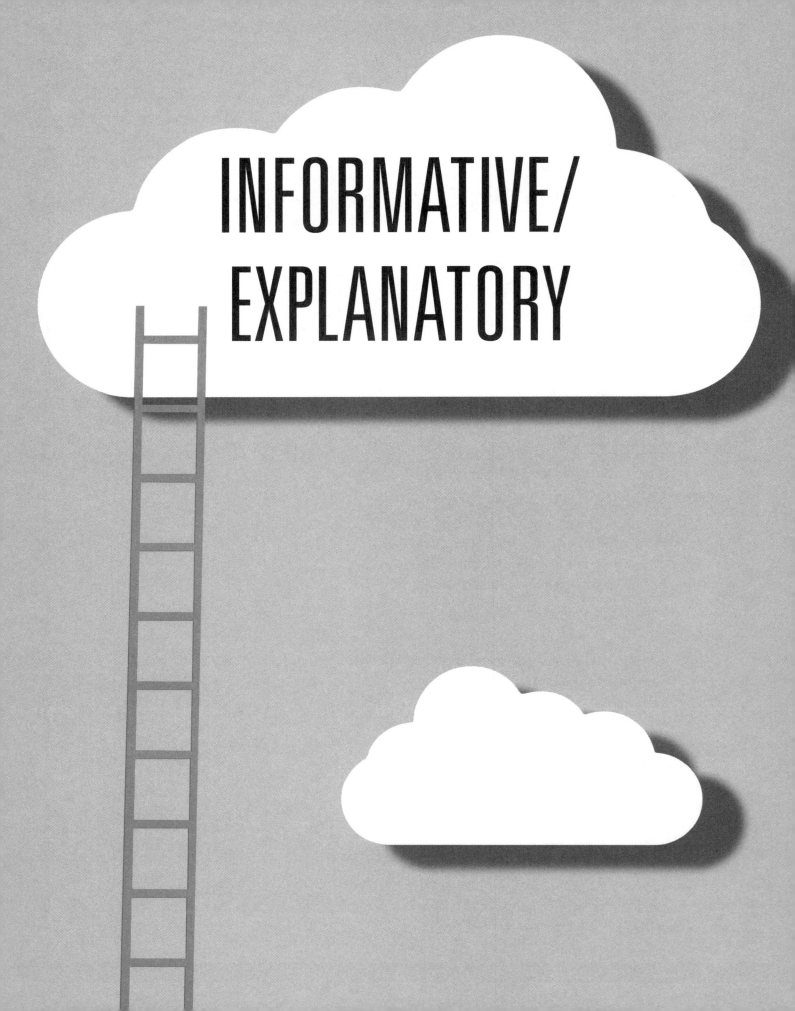

A Note About Informative/ Explanatory Writing

While argument is based on opinion or belief, informative/explanatory writing is more about explaining a concept, clarifying a process, or describing how something is made or how it works. Most analysis falls into this category, because a writer looks at something by examining its parts. For this reason, we include response to literature in this section.

In the real world, informative writing happens because someone is asking for information. Someone needs to know something or to understand something better. The writer addresses the topic to clear up some kind of confusion.

In academic writing, that situation is simulated but still imaginable.

All compelling writing contains clearly written information and explanations. Arguments cannot be convincing without information; narratives won't sustain a reader without clear explanations.

But in testing situations, the categories are so artificially separated that we recognize the need to strengthen the components of these kinds of writing and attempt to separate them for you. You may notice, naturally, some genre overlap in the student pieces and wonder why we didn't place a piece in a different section of the book. Know that that's because many of these student pieces were not written under rigid testing situations to fit into a testing genre but as part of a varied and rich year's worth of teaching in a classroom.

We marvel at classrooms that produce beautiful analysis. One gorgeous example is the work of Annie Adams, a high school student who analyzed *Of Mice and Men* with a painting, a poem, and an explanation of her thinking about the literary work. Her pieces end this section. They will take your breath away.

Sharing Culture Through Special Events

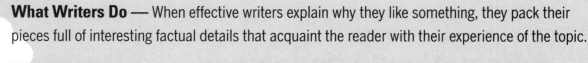

What Writers Do — When effective writers explain why they like something, they pack their pieces full of interesting factual details that acquaint the reader with their experience of the topic.

What This Writer Does — Arik breaks down his favorite holiday into different parts and carefully explains each one. Rather than telling us over and over that he likes it and it is fun, he *shows* us, providing a rich body of information that builds a strong picture of the holiday.

Activity for your class:

1. Pass out copies to students and ask them to number Arik's paragraphs.

2. In groups or with partners, write a few words on a sticky note that identify the topic of each paragraph.

3. While students are working, draw a chart with the empty text structure boxes on the board or on chart paper.

4. Have students post their sticky notes on each box on the chart and explain what they wrote.

5. Tell students that they have now analyzed Arik's piece and have captured a text structure that they can use anytime.

Challenge for students:

Pick out a special event that you enjoy and try writing a piece using the new text structure.

All About an Event

How the event started	What we eat and why	One object we use	Something we read or sing	Why I like it so much

All About Purim

We celebrate Purim because Haman made a decree. He said, "To kill all Jews." Esther told Achashverosh that she was a Jew. Before that she fasted for 3 days. Then Achashverosh hung Haman. By fasting, it was a way of praying to G-d.

On Purim, we eat cookies called Hamantashen. They remind us of Haman's ears, pocket, and/or hat. Haman was in charge and everyone was scared of him. But Hashem flipped everything over and Haman was scared. That is why we eat Hamantashen.

We use groggers when we read the Megillah. We sound the groggers when we hear Haman's name. The groggers are very loud. Haman was a very wicked man. Haman was so wicked we make noise to forget his name.

Esther and Mordechai wrote the Megillah. The Megillah is the whole Purim story. The Megillah has Hebrew words. I love the Megillah because it has action. The Megillah is written by a sofer. A sofer is someone who is specially trained to write the Torah or Megillah.

I like Purim because we read the Megillah. I like it because we put costumes on. I love Purim. It is fun. We play a lot of stuff. We will make a play at my shul. I like the part in the story when Haman gets hanged. ☆

Explaining a Historical Context

What Writers Do — Writers use a variety of organizational patterns to explain how things have happened in history.

What This Writer Does —In this short explanation, Angelica explains how and why the Magna Carta was signed.

Activity for your class:

1. Read the piece together with the class.

2. Have the text structure, below, written or projected where students can see it. Invite students to pose a question based on each box in the text structure below (for example, *1st box—Why did this event [writing the Magna Carta] happen?*).

3. Discuss whether Angelica answered the questions in her essay.

4. On sticky notes, have students write additional questions that they have about the topic.

5. Choose some questions that could become additional details in this piece. Add them as boxes to the text structure (for example, *new box—What does the Magna Carta say?*).

Challenge for students:

Think of a document that you consider important. Try using the text structure below to explain what caused that document to be created. See if you can anticipate any questions that your readers might have when they read your explanation. Add details to your piece that answer those questions.

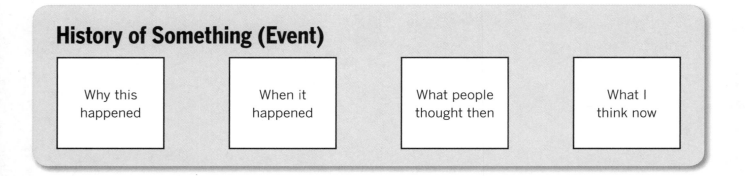

History of Something (Event)

Why this happened	When it happened	What people thought then	What I think now

---

The Magna Carta

King John (the king) was very bad at being a king. John had many bigger brothers but they all died. So John was crowned king. He often forgot to do important things, got mixed up with his paperwork, and lacked protection for the people.

The Magna Carta was written in the Middle Ages. It happened late in the Middle Ages in the 13th century to be exact.

People thought King John was a menace of a king, so they established the Magna Carta which means "Great Wish," and it was a great wish from the people.

Now most people think that the signing of the Magna Carta was an important event in history. It affects our government, how it works, how we are controlled, and how extreme laws could be. The Magna Carta was and still is very important. ☆

Using Compound Predicates in a Series

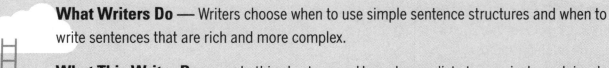

What Writers Do — Writers choose when to use simple sentence structures and when to write sentences that are rich and more complex.

What This Writer Does — In this short essay, Hannah uses lists to concisely explain what she's observed about animal habits. These lists form multiple predicates.

Activity for your class:

1. Project the essay or post it on chart paper. Read the piece aloud.

2. Read it again more slowly. Ask students to raise their hands when they see a multiple predicate (for example, in the second sentence, *"lounge, sleep, and generally lack enthusiasm;"* circle this collection and write numbers 1, 2, 3 over the three parts.).

3. Continue to circle and number multiple predicates.

4. Now read aloud the essay without those sentences. Ask students to explain the difference in what they hear.

Challenge for students:

Choose a piece you've written. Look for places to add to your examples using multiple predicates the same way Hannah did. How does this change your essay?

The Story of My Thinking

| I used to think... | But then this happened... | So now I think... |

Towering Hearts of Animals

What I used to think is that animals are ordinary. And they don't do anything but lounge, sleep, and generally lack enthusiasm.

But I purchased a puppy that was ten weeks old. And I observed her. She dashed when I chased her. She played with her toys. She nibbled my toes, ears, and fingers. She pulled my hair. This wasn't just a plain old animal. It was my very own best friend.

I kissed her on the forehead when I was going to sleep. And her soft wet tongue licked me on my cheek.

So now I think that animals have towering hearts, and don't just lounge, sleep and do nothing. They bolt, play and nibble. They do everything every day. ☆

Analyzing Characters by Writing Letters Between Them

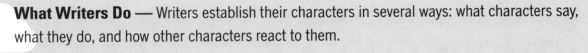

> **What Writers Do** — Writers establish their characters in several ways: what characters say, what they do, and how other characters react to them.
>
> **What This Writer Does** — In this delightful exchange of letters, Karsyn and Hannah demonstrate their understanding of two characters from the book *Matilda* by Roald Dahl.

Activity for your class:

1. Pass out copies. Have two students play the roles of the two characters and read aloud their letters and responses.

2. Ask students to draw arrows between the characters' questions and answers to each other.

3. Next, ask them to draw arrows between the characters' responses to each other's comments.

4. Share what you notice about these patterns, about the characters' personalities, and about their reactions to each other.

Challenge for students:

Choose two characters from a story or novel and write letters between the two. Make sure to include the same kinds of questions/answers and comments/responses as in the sample. Check the text structure below to help you organize your letters.

Letter Exchange Between Two Characters

Letter from 1st character	Letter back from 2nd character	Letter back from 1st character	Repeat as much as you want

---

Part II. Informative/Explanatory

Dear Miss Honey,

Don't you think your aunt is just a little bit sassy? I think that she is more than sassy. I think that she is spiteful and supernatural, totally unlike you because you are delightful and gorgeous. I would love to come visit sometime. But when shall I see you again?

Yours Truely, Matilda

Dear Matilda,

Those are nice things you said about me. I think Aunt Trunchbull is worst than that. Do you know what she has done to me, well never mind let's not go there. I wanted to know what does your dad do to those cars?

Yours truly, Ms. Honey

Dear Miss Honey,

Well, first, he takes the bumper (if it has fallen off) and uses "super super glue" to glue it back on. Then he uses a drill (that spins backwards) to make the mileage go down to make the car brand new. But then, he paints the car with paint that is bright and shiny. That is why I think The Trunchbull came home so early from the gym. Because of the mileage of course.

Yours, Matilda

Dear Matilda,

Wow! He really does that? If I were him I would actually try to fix the cars and not use "super super glue" to put the bumper back on. What does he do to the engine? Does he do anything to that?

Extremely curious, Miss Honey

Dear Miss Honey,

I forgot this in my other letters. I wrote a little script about The Trunchbull and why she is so mean, so here goes.

Announcer: So Agatha, why are you so mean?

Agatha: Well when I was little my parents would lock me in a box. But one day I snuck out and randomly found five tickets to Las Vegas. I was so suprized I actually screamed "Las Vegas?!" and a party pulled up, grabbed the tickets, and then drove off. That's why.

Announcer: Wow! What a story!

The End

Yours, Matilda

P.S. with the engine he puts sawdust in it.

Dear Best Student EVER,

I wish that script was true, but sadly it isn't. Why does he put the sawdust in the engine? That is terrible that he does that. I wonder how much he made today? By the way, where is your mother during the day?

With lots more questions, Miss Honey

P.S. SAWDUST? Are you serious?

Dear Miss Honey,

We must hurry with these letters. My mother and father are getting really curious about what I am doing. If I tell them I am afraid I will get a woopen. Should I tell them, or tell them to mind their own business?

Confused, Matilda

Dear Matilda,

Don't tell them anything. Well, if you want to tell the truth do, but you might get a woopen. If you don't you might get in more trouble. Late for my tea and toast. Got to run. I'm really famished right now!

In a hurry, Miss Honey

Miss Honey,

I am serious, he really does put sawdust in the engine. My father probably made over 10,000 dollars. He always lies about the prices. It is sad isn't it? Oh, and about my mother, every day she leaves about 7:30 for bingo games. I get so annoyed!

Furiously, Matilda

Dear Matilda,

Really 10,000 dollars? Got to run. See you tomorrow at school Ready for the weekly test?

Love, Miss Honey

P.S. Do you have to feed yourself and make your lunch?

Miss Honey,

If you must leave for tea, I am <u>very</u> fine with that. Speaking for myself, I am very parched. Goodbye! Yes, I do make my lunch! And I'm ready for the test. ☆

Good but parched, Matilda

Tracking a Changing Thought Process

What Writers Do — Writers sometimes explain how their basic beliefs are tempered by experiences.

What This Writer Does — Isabella explains how, after the death of her dog, her thinking about death changed and she arrived at a new understanding.

Activity for your class:

1. Read the piece aloud after distributing copies.

2. Have students draw three panels for a storyboard on a large piece of paper.

3. In the first and third panels, draw the narrator with a thought bubble.

4. In the second panel, draw the scene from Isabella's second paragraph.

5. Write the narrator's beliefs in the beginning and ending thought bubbles.

Challenge for students:

Think of an experience you had that changed the way you think about something. First draw a similar storyboard, and then write a short essay explaining the change. You can use the text structure below.

The Story of My Thinking

| I used to think... | But then this happened... | So now I think... |

Death Can Actually Happen

I used to think that people could not really die from a heart attack or a stroke. I thought that they could only really die from gun shots or a knife in their heart.

But this happened when my dad and my dog Meatball Maximuss and I were walking to my school to drop me off. Meatball was getting really tired. So after they dropped me off my dad said to Meatball, "okay you can rest Meatball while I call Bella's mom Alicia." Meatball did but then my dad realized that he was coughing up blood and then he started falling asleep like after a cat drinks milk. And then when my mom came to go see what was going on...It was too late. My poor baby Meatball was dead. My dad tried everything to bring him back to life. But then we had to bury him and we put a cross on his grave made out of brick.

So now I think even if someone or something in your life dies they will always still live in your heart. I know because my dog Meatball died but whenever I go in my backyard I still think of him since he is in a better place now. ☆

Responding to Literature: Questioning the Author (Part I)

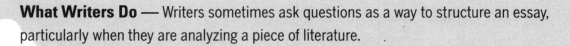

What Writers Do — Writers sometimes ask questions as a way to structure an essay, particularly when they are analyzing a piece of literature.

What This Writer Does —As she read *I Am the Ice Worm* by Mary Ann Easley, Maggie found several passages that made her want to ask the author questions. She explained those to create an interesting and thought-provoking literary analysis.

Activity for your class:

1. Read the piece as your students follow along on their own copies.

2. Project or write on chart paper the text structure below, "Questioning the Author."

3. Have students find the three places in the essay where Maggie wished she could ask the author a question and circle each one (for example, I'd ask her why she wrote *"it looked like the moon."*).

4. Next, ask them to circle Maggie's introduction and conclusion.

5. Explain that this is one way to create a literary analysis of a novel or article. Discuss with students whether they think this model might be useful to them.

Challenge for students:

Consider something interesting that you have read recently. Maggie used fiction; try it with nonfiction, too. Find places in the text that made you wish you could ask the author something. Use the text structure "Questioning the Author" to explain your thinking as you read the selection.

Full Analysis Using "Questioning the Author"

Intro	+ (	Questioning the Author			× 3) +	Conclusion
		I'd ask ____	Because I read "____"	I thought ____		

Allison Atwood's Adventure

Every writer has many ways of getting a reader's attention. They make characters that people instantly fall in love with just like Allison Atwood. In *I am the Ice Worm*, written by Mary Ann Easley, she uses not only characters we fall in love with, but she also uses surprises to keep me "hooked" on her book. *I am the Ice Worm* is about fourteen year old Allison Atwood who is flying to visit her mom in Alaska when her plane crashes and her pilot gets killed. She is trapped in the snow until an Inupiat man finds her.

While Allison is flying she looks out the window and thinks: *"The landscape below looked like the moon. There wasn't a single tree, not a building or road, no sign of life at all."* There are a few things I would tell or ask Mary Ann Easley about this particular section. I'd tell her first and foremost I loved your book! I thought it was well written. I'd ask her why she wrote *"it looked like the moon?"* I read *"It looked like the moon."* I thought they coordinated the flight wrong and they were in space! In this part the author used astonishing images to keep me reading this novel.

Right after Allison crashed in her plane she was so thankful she didn't crash, went to the cockpit, and thought: *"The coldest wind I've ever felt in my life."* I asked myself why the author wrote this because she could've gone to colder places. Allison thought she crashed in Alaska. In this section the author used suspense to keep me hooked.

At the beginning of the plane crash Allison used this description: *"The engine coughed, then died. Utter silence. Only the sound of my heart. We fell through the dark, descending down, too fast. I shut my eyes, waited for the crash. I waited to die."* I thought WOW! That is very well written and very descriptive. When I read *"The engine coughed"* I thought it really meant it coughed; then I read

on and found out that the engine died and then I realized this was opening up to the plane crash.

I'm a very picky reader! I usually judge a book by its cover or by the first paragraph. Then I picked up the book and the cover didn't look so interesting but then I read the first paragraph and I was hooked! The story was well written and much descripted. In this book I loved the suspense of, will she be okay? Will she be stranded forever? Mary Anne Easley's writing affected me not only as a reader but as a writer and I know she will change you too. ☆

Responding to Literature: Questioning the Author (Part II)

What Writers Do — Writers sometimes record the mental conversations they have as they read someone else's writing.

What This Writer Does — In his essay, Josh imagines a conversation with author Rick Riordan, and he pinpoints three surprising and zany places in his book, all of which cause delight.

Activity for your class:

1. Read the piece together with the class.

2. Ask students to use highlighters to find:
   - green—quotations from the book
   - yellow—Josh's reactions to the quotations
   - pink—the overall effect that these had on Josh

Challenge for students:

Write a similar response to a book you've read, using quotations and reactions to quotations to show how the book impacted you as a reader.

Full Analysis Using "Questioning the Author"

Intro	+ (	Questioning the Author			× 3) +	Conclusion
		I'd ask ____	Because I read "____"	I thought ____		

Suspense, Humor, and Comedy
All In One Book: *The Last Olympian*

Writers use lots of tricks to keep readers reading, like suspense, humor, and other stuff. In *The Last Olympian*, Rick Riordan keeps his readers reading by using a killer creative beginning and crazy chapter names. In the story, Percy Jackson seeks revenge against the underworld.

If I could have a conversation with Rick Riordan, I'd ask him how he came up with such a ridiculously amazing start to a book. When I read *"The end of the world started when a Pegasus landed on the roof of my car"* (p. 5), I thought okay, I'm going to love this book. This is the first thing I noticed about how creative his writing is. And I was hooked. How often have I ever read one sentence and known I was going to read the entire book? Not that often.

I wish I could ask Rick Riordan what's up with the crazy chapter names too. I read "My Parents Go Commando" which was the name of chapter 18 (p.312), and I thought Percy's parents were Greek gods, so that does make sense.

I'd ask Rick Riordan, "You drove WHAT into a tree?!?" when I read the title for chapter 5: "I Drove My Dog Into a Tree" (79). I thought that was crazy because normally you'd be driving a car, so it shocked me and kept me interested.

Rick Riordan's stories are a little predictable, and they would benefit from more suspense, but I read them happily because of all the craziness I love in them. ☆

Conversing With an Imagined Listener

What Writers Do — Sometimes people discuss a problem with a friend, who listens and reacts as friends do, asking questions and listening some more. Writers may write about a problem, almost as though a conversation is going on, and work through it that way.

What This Writer Does — In a letter to her grandmother, Karishma vents about something that is bothering her. By the time she gets to the end of her letter, she has figured out a plan—and revealed her thought processes to her readers.

Activity for your class:

1. Distribute copies and read the piece aloud as students follow along.

2. Have partners read the piece aloud again with one person pausing after each sentence, giving the other person a chance to improvise questions from the grandmother (for example, *"I had the worst day today!"* [Q. What happened?] *"Schools really shouldn't have a mandatory music class."* [Q. How's your grade, honey?]).

3. As they read, have them jot down some of the questions the grandmother might be asking and reread it as a dialogue.

Challenge for students:

Think about a problem that's frustrating you and write a letter to someone you trust, venting about it. See if you can imagine what they would say, and let your side of the conversation continue. Does it lead you to a plan for solving it? You might want to use the text structure below.

Venting a Problem/Finding a Solution

My frustration about something	One detail about how bad it is	What I don't understand about it	My plan for solving it

Part II. Informative/Explanatory

Wednesday, March 9, 2011

Dear Grandma,

I had the worst day today! The only thing that ruined my day was music class. I did not want to play Jolly Old Saint Nicholas or Ode to Joy for an hour! I would rather have a theater class or an art class. That way I will at least enjoy school and I will have fun. Schools really shouldn't have a mandatory music class.

My grade average in music class went down from a one hundred to a ninety-three just because I wasn't participating, and the only reason I wasn't participating was because I do not enjoy music class as much as I would enjoy a theater class!

I really don't get why they spend so much money on the instruments when some of the students, like me, don't even like music class. The guitars themselves cost about five hundred dollars each! I just wish we had more options. Maybe I should recommend that to the principal and get a bunch of kids to sign a petition. That will convince him to provide a theater class! Yes! That's exactly what I'll do! Thanks Grandma! ☆

Love,

Maria

Explaining a Concept From the Point of View of a Character

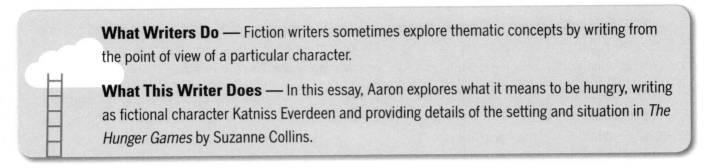

What Writers Do — Fiction writers sometimes explore thematic concepts by writing from the point of view of a particular character.

What This Writer Does — In this essay, Aaron explores what it means to be hungry, writing as fictional character Katniss Everdeen and providing details of the setting and situation in *The Hunger Games* by Suzanne Collins.

Activity for your class:

1. Read the piece aloud after distributing copies.

2. Ask students to find and circle these chunks of text:

   - physical descriptions of hunger
   - a memory about not having hunger
   - all about digging through the trash for food
   - the change in the family's situation and what it means in terms of hunger

3. Discuss how these fit the text structure below.

Challenge for students:

Aaron explores hunger, drawing details from Katniss's situation in the novel. Try explaining the meaning of another abstract word (*courage, self-doubt, loneliness,* or *perseverance*) from the point of view of a character in a book you've read. You might try using the text structure below.

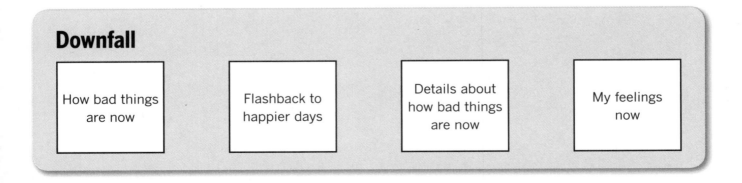

Downfall

| How bad things are now | Flashback to happier days | Details about how bad things are now | My feelings now |

Hunger Games

It seems like all my life I have only known hunger. The loud rumbling in my stomach reminds me how hungry I really am. I see people die almost every day here. It is because we are all hungry and no one cares. The Capitol, they just make me mad. They don't care about me. They don't care about anyone. The Capitol only cares about the Capitol.

I can remember a time when my father was alive. We were still poor, but we had food to eat. I didn't have to worry about starving to death. All I had to worry about was being a kid. Playing and having fun. I learned so many things from him. He was my shining star. I miss him terribly.

Life has gotten to be so hard. I am sick of digging in the trash for food. If I do find something it is a small amount. I wonder if it will be enough to help me make it through the next day. The smells I smell are gagging and the thought of what I might find makes me even sicker to my stomach. But I know I have to survive so I can take care of me and my family.

Oh no! My sister was chosen to be the contribute. It was suicide. She is too young to have to fight this fight. She had no idea how to take care of herself. I have always been the one to take care of her. I yelled "I volunteer as contribute." I stepped up. I thought, I can do this. I am so scared but I am relieved that my sister will be okay. Even if I die, it will at least be over. No more digging in the trash, no more horrible smells, and no more hunger. ☆

Writing About Clues That Reveal a Situation

What Writers Do — Writers sometimes write about a confusing time in their life and about their mixed feelings as they realize something bad is happening.

What This Writer Does — Caleb masterfully explains what he suspected, what he saw, and what he learned as he discovered his parents were divorcing. Though he included his own clear pain and reactions, his writing remains focused on the clues he witnessed, allowing his audience to "read between the lines."

Activity for your class:

1. Invite a volunteer to read the piece aloud after passing out copies.

2. Have students highlight the following parts:

   - yellow—what the author suspected
   - green—the clues he witnessed
   - blue—the news at the end

Challenge for students:

Think of a time you suspected something was going on (and it can be something happy, funny, surprising, or sad), and see if you can list some specific clues that helped you "read between the lines." Using Caleb's structure, write what you suspected and when you found out the truth.

Clues and Confirmation

What I was afraid was happening	Some clues that told me this	Some more clues that told me	How I finally knew the truth

     Part II. Informative/Explanatory

I Wish I Was Wrong

I was certain that I was right. All the screaming and name calling was a ginormous hint. I hated to think it, but I was confident that my parents were going to get a divorce. Every night my mom would slumber with me while my greedy father slept on their extremely comfy water bed. She would enumerate that it was all okay. It would work out and they would be delighted to see each other again. I couldn't believe her, though. I was too stubborn and I was sure that they would sign the dreaded papers. For six weeks I had to dwell like that. "I hate you!" she would scream as she malled the wall with a heavy object. I recall one day that I walked into the bathroom and my mom slung a hairdryer at the bathtub. My dad didn't seem to take it very serious. Sometimes he would laugh. To see my mom and dad struggle with each other all the time was horrible.

I hated not getting to go somewhere with both of them. I began to stay at home all the time except when going to school. My parents never ventured to the same place. If mom went to the grocery store, dad and I sojourned at home. If dad arrived at a baseball game, I wasn't with him, I was at home with mom. I was so depressed that I wouldn't ever play outside. I would remain in my room and watch television. The worst part of it all was not being able to spot them out together. They were always seperate. It had to be. I couldn't think of a way that they wouldn't compromise on a divorce! They were so fed up with each other that they even started cooking seperate meals. On some days Mom and I would eat at 11:30 and dad at 12:30. On other days dad and I would eat at 11:30 and mom at 12:30. It alternated. Before, my mom would cook one meal for all of us, but now they would cook for themselves and me, depending on if they had me that day or if they didn't. This has been the only situation so far that I wished I wasn't right. I loved both of my parents and I wanted deeply for them to remain together and be happy. I wanted new siblings, especially a brother that would look up to me for help and advice. I wanted to teach him how to hunt, fish, and many things, but I didn't think that would happen anytime soon.

My parents were probably going to get a divorce. I kept trying to tell myself that I was wrong, but when I got the unbearable news that my dad was moving in with my grandma my heart sank. I was right. They were divorcing. On February 22nd my parents signed the papers, making it official that my mom no longer had the same last name as me. I now desire to know what it feels like to have two parents instead of four. I wish I was wrong back then, but I love my new parents and I will always admire my dad for never hitting my mom. ☆

Writing a Letter Using Second-Person Point of View

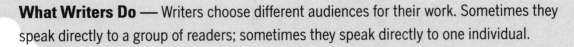

What Writers Do — Writers choose different audiences for their work. Sometimes they speak directly to a group of readers; sometimes they speak directly to one individual.

What This Writer Does — Instead of an essay, Sarah chooses to write in letter form. This allows her to discuss an important friendship using second person (you) instead of third (she or he), speaking directly to her friend.

Activity for your class:

1. Have students read the piece aloud with a partner or small group.

2. Discuss: Are the sentences about the person? to the person? or both?

3. Now ask students to rewrite one paragraph writing in third-person essay form. How would this piece seem different if it were not written as a letter? Why do you think the author chose to direct it to her friend instead of writing a third-person essay?

Challenge for students:

Think about your friends. Choose one of them and write about your friendship. You may choose to put your thoughts into letter form directly *to* them, or into third-person form, *about* them. You can use the text structure below if you wish. (Switch the pronouns to third person if you need to—*one moment* she *taught me an important lesson.*)

Development of a Friendship

My wrong first impression	Moment of bonding	One moment you taught me an important lesson	Another moment you taught me an important lesson	Ways you've become my most important friend

Dear Dalia,

Do you remember when we were kids and we were both really bossy? We used to fight over who was right and who was wrong. Even though we were kids we still acted like we knew everything. But we didn't know that we would be the answer to each other's problems.

When we first met you were six and I was turning seven. I was outside coloring on the sidewalk. You came up to me and said, "Chalk is for the sidewalk and markers are for paper." No offense, but right then and there I wanted to slap you. Have you ever heard of first impressions? Because yours wasn't the best. You probably felt the same way with me. Don't worry, I would be freaked out too if I saw a kid coloring the sidewalk with Crayola markers.

Do you remember how your dad would come home drunk and yell at your mom? I remember it like it was crystal clear. Every time they would fight, you, your sister and I would pray from under your bed. Thank you for showing me that I was never alone. Now I know that God is always with us.

Field day at school was coming up and your dad said you couldn't go. There was no reason for you not to be able to go except your dad. He had to make everything put you down. It was like he was allergic to happiness. He would always say things like, "You're so ugly, you're as ugly as your fat mom," or, "No guy would ever like you." What's really sad is he put me down too. The first time we met he said, "So you're Dalia's little fat friend." It was time for us to defend ourselves.

"Dad, why don't you be nice for a change? Why do you always put me down? Just because you're not happy doesn't mean you have to ruin our lives because of it," clamored Dalia. For once he said he was sorry. And I felt great knowing I changed your relationship toward your dad.

From you teaching me that I am not alone, from me teaching you about courage. We complete each other. Even when we were kids we always knew something that the other one didn't. You are the nucleus to my cell. You are the missing piece to my puzzle. You are my best friend. ☆

Love always,

Sarah Cavanaugh

Using Personification to Turn an Abstract Concept Into a Colorful Character

What Writers Do — Writers use literary devices like metaphors, similes, and personification in their writing. Sometimes the entire piece is an extended metaphor or an extended personification.

What This Writer Does — Shanice, Kaleb, and Tre each chose an abstract concept or feeling and personified it, creating fascinating details about those concepts-as-people and their lives.

Activity for your class:

1. Read the pieces.

2. Invite students to choose one of the descriptions and draw a sketch of it, showing as many details from the writing as they can.

3. Share sketches with a gallery walk, discussing similarities and differences.

Challenge for students:

Choose an abstract concept or feeling (e.g., hope, anticipation, anger) and write an extended personification about it in the style that these students used. Draw a sketch to go with your piece. Use the text structure below or create one of your own.

Personifying an Abstract

_____ is what kind of person	What she or he does around others	What effect she or he has on others	One thing she or he does

(Inspired by J. Ruth Gendler's *A Book of Qualities*)

Personification Writings, Grade 7
Inspired by J. Ruth Gendler's *A Book of Qualities*

Fear

Fear is a little girl who hides under the cover at night from the monsters under her bed. She tells her mom, but her mom says it's going to be alright. So Fear keeps the light on so the monsters won't get her at night.

—Shanice Hubbard

Inspiration

Inspiration was wonderful. Always showing others the way around the block. He created masterpieces, and the people who made them. Inspiration gave the world that little spark of color around the edges to ignite the film of imagination. He painted with the brushes of creation, and the colors of the people. He led the world to greatness. Gave people the ability to be individuals...not another passerby, like countless others. Inspiration turned the dullness to light and magnificent colors. He turned the frowns upside down, and sometimes sideways. Inspiration gave way to Creativity.

—Kaleb Benish

Faith

Faith believes that someday her dad will come back from the war. Her cat has a heart problem, but Faith knows the cat will get well. Faith sits next to me when a loved one is dying, whispering in my ear that everything will be fine. Faith is my best friend when there is no one else who is willing to be. Faith is everybody's friend, even though they can't see her. ☆

—Tre Staples

115

Writing a Graphic Book Review

What Writers Do — When readers like a book, they share information about it with other readers, sometimes by writing a book review.

What This Writer Does — In her graphic book review, Batya offers intriguing glimpses into Rick Riordan's *Mission Road*. The information she provides will help other readers decide whether they'd like to read it, too.

Activity for your class:

1. Ask your students to look at the elements included on the page and then read each section.

2. Invite them to go on a treasure hunt for the following sections. Circle and label each one:
   - quotations from the book and Batya's reactions to them
   - a place where the book's genre is mentioned
   - information about the setting, characters, and plot
   - information about the publication of the book
   - her star-rating
   - information about the reviewer

Challenge for students:

Create a similar review of a book you have read, either in graphic form, with illustrations, like Batya's, or in another form. Use the text structure below to be sure you provide a variety of relevant information in your review.

Book Review

Information about publication	Favorite lines, with commentary	Information about characters, setting, plot	Recommendation

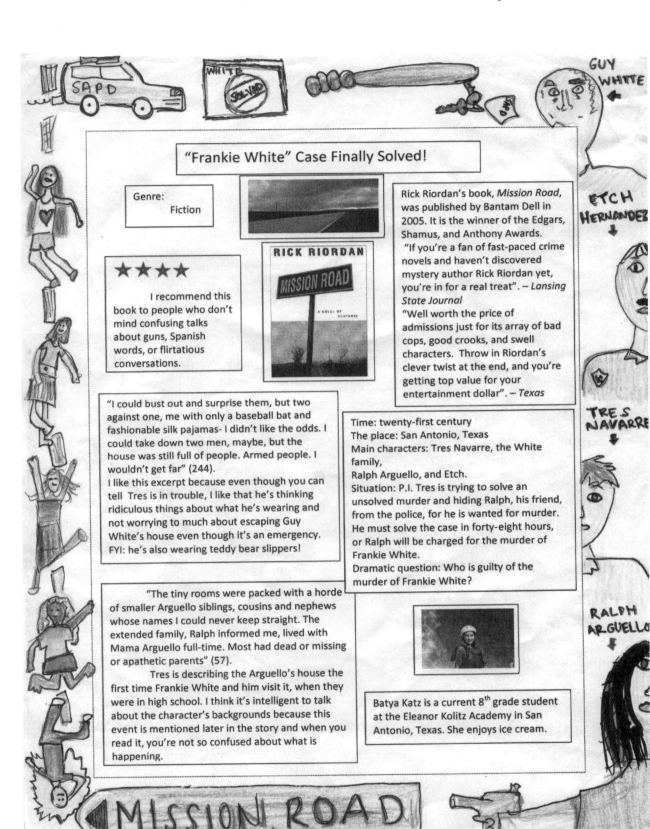

"Frankie White" Case Finally Solved!

Genre:
Fiction

★★★★

I recommend this book to people who don't mind confusing talks about guns, Spanish words, or flirtatious conversations.

RICK RIORDAN
MISSION ROAD
A NOVEL OF SUSPENSE

Rick Riordan's book, *Mission Road*, was published by Bantam Dell in 2005. It is the winner of the Edgars, Shamus, and Anthony Awards.
"If you're a fan of fast-paced crime novels and haven't discovered mystery author Rick Riordan yet, you're in for a real treat". – *Lansing State Journal*
"Well worth the price of admissions just for its array of bad cops, good crooks, and swell characters. Throw in Riordan's clever twist at the end, and you're getting top value for your entertainment dollar". – *Texas*

"I could bust out and surprise them, but two against one, me with only a baseball bat and fashionable silk pajamas- I didn't like the odds. I could take down two men, maybe, but the house was still full of people. Armed people. I wouldn't get far" (244).
I like this excerpt because even though you can tell Tres is in trouble, I like that he's thinking ridiculous things about what he's wearing and not worrying to much about escaping Guy White's house even though it's an emergency. FYI: he's also wearing teddy bear slippers!

Time: twenty-first century
The place: San Antonio, Texas
Main characters: Tres Navarre, the White family,
Ralph Arguello, and Etch.
Situation: P.I. Tres is trying to solve an unsolved murder and hiding Ralph, his friend, from the police, for he is wanted for murder. He must solve the case in forty-eight hours, or Ralph will be charged for the murder of Frankie White.
Dramatic question: Who is guilty of the murder of Frankie White?

"The tiny rooms were packed with a horde of smaller Arguello siblings, cousins and nephews whose names I could never keep straight. The extended family, Ralph informed me, lived with Mama Arguello full-time. Most had dead or missing or apathetic parents" (57).
Tres is describing the Arguello's house the first time Frankie White and him visit it, when they were in high school. I think it's intelligent to talk about the character's backgrounds because this event is mentioned later in the story and when you read it, you're not so confused about what is happening.

Batya Katz is a current 8th grade student at the Eleanor Kolitz Academy in San Antonio, Texas. She enjoys ice cream.

Analyzing Literature: Focusing on Character Tension

What Writers Do — Writers sometimes create tension by having their characters worry and fret about things they don't understand.

What This Writer Does — Eileen shows how a character in *The Help* is tormented by something she doesn't know.

Activity for your class:

1. Pass out copies and ask students to read the piece silently.

2. Have partners or small groups reread it, using highlighters to find the following:

   • yellow—words and phrases that show what the character knows

   • green—words and phrases that show what she does *not* know

Challenge for students:

Think of a character from a book or story you have read recently, especially a character who is struggling with something. Make a t-chart showing things the character does know and things the character does not know. Write a paper about this using the text structure below.

One Thing the Character Would Like to Know About

She or he sometimes wonders about...	She or he knows that _____ (and how)	She or he also knows _____ (and how)	She or he can't figure out how...	So she or he plans to...

The Quest for Constantine

In Kathryn Stockett's novel *The Help*, something is tugging at Skeeter. Skeeter Phelan sometimes wonders about where her childhood maid, Constantine is. Skeeter was closer to Constantine than her own mother. They understood each other. They were meant to be a set of two, a dynamic duo. But then Constantine left her. Skeeter needs to now why.

Skeeter is just more concerned that Constantine had the audacity to leave her, after all they had been through together! Constantine had been more than the help; she had been family.

Skeeter is also aware of the fact that Constantine's daughter, whatever her name might be, could have something to do with Constantine's hasty departure. So of course, Skeeter must find out some more information on Constantine's daughter, this unexpected, problematic figure. Skeeter starts to question Aibeleen, a friend's maid, about Constantine's whereabouts. Aibileen isn't willing to share her facts.

It is just quizzical to Skeeter that someone so close could leave her so far away. It hurts that she didn't leave her a letter. They always used to write each other. That was then, this is now.

That is why Skeeter plans to find out why Constantine left her. No matter how difficult emotionally compromising getting the information she needs will be, she needs to find out why or how Constantine left her. And that is just one thing Eugenia "Skeeter" Phelan would like to know about.

This is a dilemma. She has spent two whole months crying herself to sleep over this. Constantine and Skeeter had a special bond and it put extreme emotional strain on Skeeter when she left. Skeeter can only wonder about how Constantine feels. Skeeter deserves to know the truth because Constantine was closest to her. I don't think that Skeeter's mother will ever realize just how special Constantine was to Skeeter. Skeeter's mother is being selfish from barring the truth. Skeeter is a grown adult and she deserves a basic human right: the truth. ☆

Responding to Literature: Characters Conversing About a Problem

What Writers Do — Writers may explore literary elements such as characterization in forms that go beyond a traditional essay.

What This Writer Does — Gertrude crafts an exchange of letters between two fictional characters from two different books. One character poses an important question, and the other character advises.

Activity for your class:

1. After distributing copies, choose volunteers to read the two different letters aloud.

2. Have students circle and label the actual question ("Q") in the first letter. Have them do the same for the answer ("A") they find in the second letter.

   (Q. "I need your help to find, and kill, the author of these notes." A. "...of course I'll help you.")

3. Using two different colors, ask students to find and highlight details that provide the reader with information about each character's situation.

4. Using the author's blurb, circle the sentence that explains what the two characters have in common (*someone is after both of them*).

Challenge for students:

Think of two characters from a single book or from two different books you've read recently, as Gertrude did. Choose one character that has a problem and a second character that has experienced a similar problem and could offer advice. Try writing a question-and-advice pair of letters using the text structure below.

Conversation Between Characters

Question from one character	Answer from another character	Author's blurb: why you chose those characters

Letters Between Book Characters

Dear Gale, (Hunger Games)

The contents of this letter are clandestine. It's best if we keep it on the DL. Let me inform you of my current situation: my feet are pacing, I'm seeing blood, and I'm thinking that I need your help. You are known to be intrepid and erudite in the skill of killing. I am a demure man. I am no social extrovert. However, I am receiving notes. In my car, in the mail, on my computer…they're everywhere. These letters contain ultimatums, dilemmas if you will. To help your understanding, I must decide who dies by deciding who lives. I need your help to find, and kill, the author of these notes. This creep finds death droll. He is passionately pleased by pleading people. He finds that having me in his sick game is an added bonus. You're the only one who can help me with this arduous task. Your knowledge of hunting will be helpful. When you hunt, your feet become air, you see what I can't, and you think like a predator. I'm gonna need that. Plus, you're affable and will be willing to do the job. Anyways, what should my first step be? Your call. You know everything. I'll just be there to inform you of the details. I may be dolorous and dreary. That's only because my wife is in a coma and people are dying on my accord. So will you come down to Napa Valley and help me catch a murderer? Afterwards, we could grab a beer at the place where I bartend…

Call me whenever,

Billy Wiles (*Velocity*)

P.S. Is Katniss as pretty in person as she is on the T.V.? I've always wondered…

Dear Billy, (*Velocity*)

Obviously, I've received your letter. But before we start, I have a question: I've never heard of the Napa Valley District. Where is it? Back to your problem; of course I'll help you. What are futuristic friends for? Okay. I've compiled a list of what you need to do:

- find the killer

- kill him

Easy enough? I'm just kidding. You're obviously rudimentary at these things. First, do the letters contain clues as to who the killer is? Second, is it possible that it's someone you know? Someone you work with, a friend? I'm sorry to hear about the lady that died because you couldn't make your mind up fast enough. When I get down there, I will train you until you have the physical and psychological reflexes of a puma.

Sincerely,

Gale (*Hunger Games*)

P.S. No, she's hideous in person.

Author's Blurb: First of all, I decided to incorporate Gale from *Hunger Games* and Billy from *Velocity* because I think that they're both awesome. Now, all I had to do was write a letter between them. What do they have in common? Then it hit me. Someone is after both of them. Whether it be a government or a killer. That's what spurred me to pen these letters…

Analyzing Literature: Identifying Character Conflicts

What Writers Do — Writers sometimes reveal character through scenes that illustrate conflict.

What This Writer Does — In her thoughtful essay about *The Glass Castle* by Jeannette Walls, Petronila describes several conflicts between the author and her parents, thereby revealing the character of those involved.

Activity for your class:

1. Read the piece together with the class.

2. For each body paragraph, ask students to find and highlight:
   - green—what happens (for example, *her mother tries to defend her grandmother*)
   - yellow—how Petronila interprets it (*I think this says a lot about...*)

3. In the conclusion, circle the overall impact that the conflicts between characters had on the writer of the essay (*fascinated by the author's life, wanted more from each page turn*).

Challenge for students:

Think about a book you have read in which two characters clash. Using this essay structure, write a discussion citing specific moments the way that Petronila did.

Character Clashes

Description of problem between characters	Example 1	Example 2	Example 3	What these create for the reader

Parental Insanity as Shown in
The Glass Castle

Don't you just hate it when your parents go crazy and refuse to feed you? I know we all do. However, most of us are lucky enough to have never experienced this. On the other hand, when I read *The Glass Castle*, I found the benign psychological abuse Jeanette's parents inflicted upon her intriguing. Each chapter included an ordeal with her mother that left my jaw dropping. Here are a few of them:

When Jeannette's mother (Rosemary) tries to defend her foul grandmother, she points out that each and every person possesses a respectable quality. Jeannette challenges this. She asks what Hitler's redeeming quality was. "Hitler loved dogs," Mom said without hesitation. I think this says a lot about her mother's perception of reality. Her mother had always been very trusting of people who were dodgy. For example, no matter how many times Jeannette's father beats and berates his wife, she refuses to confront her issues with him.

Another example of Rosemary's naïveté is when she believes that her daughters can take care of themselves without a strong feminine figure to look up to. She tells them that she will be spending the summer renewing her teaching degree at a state college. Instead she hangs out in the dorms and enjoys having no responsibilities. When she comes home, she informs Jeannette that it's time she "starts living life for herself." She tells the girls to get their own jobs and make their own money. Why does she always have to be the one who earns the money, she reasons. Just because she is the mother doesn't mean that she has to provide for her children, right? This left me shocked. The author had drawn me in without me realizing it. I couldn't wait to see what Rosemary would do/say next…

After this episode, I realized that her mother wasn't the only parent that was kind of…off. Her father (Rex) was always very preoccupied with ideas that he was never capable of accomplishing and get-rich-quick schemes. This came to light when Jeannette her family couldn't afford to get her braces. In fact, she had never been to a dentist. Jeannette wants to be an originator like her dad, so she makes her own braces out of a coat hanger and rubber bands. Her father encourages this instead of facing the fact that he needs to get a job and be able to provide his family with legitimate health care.

All of these situations throughout the book, and more, led me to be fascinated by the author's life. The book was an autobiography. Therefore, the author had no reason to comment on her parent's wackiness. Her nonchalant and lackadaisical demeanor left me wanting more from each page turn. ☆

Analyzing Literature: Noticing an Author's Choices

What Writers Do — When attempting to analyze what an author has done to effectively hook readers, writers may analyze the choices that author makes.

What This Writer Does — In his essay about *The Amulet of Samarkand* by Jonathan Stroud, Sylvan notes four specific things the author does to hook her, compelling her to read on.

Activity for your class:

1. Pass out copies and have students read the piece silently.

2. Ask them to write a summary sentence next to each paragraph, pinpointing what Sylvan says the author is doing to keep him hooked.

3. Read the summary sentences aloud.

4. Discuss the many examples Sylvan gives to illustrate each point.

Challenge for students:

Think of a movie you love. Write summary sentences that pinpoint specific things you loved. Try adding details from the movie to illustrate your points. How do they add up to affect you as a viewer?

Four Points and Their Effect

One thing that has this effect	Another thing that has this effect	Another thing that has this effect	One more thing that has this effect	How they all add up to create the same effect

The Amulet of Samarkand

Am I the only one who hates it when the author of the book you're reading suddenly changes characters and then you have to keep reading so you can find out what happened? That's because the author is about to reach the highpoint of the story and then changes everything so your mind is twisted and now you just want to strangle the author but you can't because you have to keep reading to find out what happens. In the Bartimaeus Trilogy, the first book, *The Amulet of Samarkand* the author changes characters every two to three chapters to keep your mind wondering and your urges hooked.

In the book most of the magicians do not have adequate protection such as shields, amulets, or a minor to medium level djinni to come to their aid. At first, I thought that with most countries having or being run by magicians, the magicians in England would never leave their house without some sort of protection. Later on in the story an elemental sphere is thrown into the ballroom containing many high ranking officials of the government, most of them either thought they were too good for protection or too dumb to think of it, but there were all blown off there lazy rumps and thrown across the room. To my surprise I expected the blast to do no damage because they should all have had a shield on that would absorb the blast cause no harm. This kept me interested because I wanted to find out why they had been so ignorant.

Adding humor to a story also tends to make the reader enjoy the little things they notice and slowly start warming up to one of the characters. When a reader likes one of the characters he wants to know more about them and or what happens to them and the only way to accomplish that is to keep reading. Near the end of the book when they are trying to stop the bad guy, Nathaniel calls Bartimaeus a demon. Bartimaeus actually is a demon but no one wants to be referred to by a derogatory name. So, to get back at him Bartimaeus won't tell Nathaniel where the defenses are until he apologizes. These cute little scenarios always make me chuckle and want to keep reading.

That moment when you find out that one of the character you thought was good turns out to be evil is one of the most important parts of a good hook on the reader. Simon Lovelace was supposed to be a part of the government and a good guy but when he steals the amulet of Samarkand, it's hard to put the book down and stop reading. Now, just because a big twist happens in the book doesn't mean the reader will like it. You have to force the reader to make the connection of what happens and the best way to do that is to lay down facts about what happened and then when finally you catch that it was Simon Lovelace, all those facts come back to you and you realize how bad that person actually is.

The only thing that makes people read your books is that hook you throw in there. Books are written to keep the reader interested and not bore them. Once the reader is bored with your book you might not get the chance to throw your hook in there. That's why if you switch up characters and use all these tips the reader is destined to love your book. ☆

Recognizing and Illustrating an Important Theme

What Writers Do — Writers may examine a common theme or truism using examples that go beyond a work of literature.

What This Writer Does — In his introduction, Ale introduces a truism, or life lesson. He then illustrates this truth using a book, a movie, and a personal friendship as examples. He concludes with an "I wonder…" statement, which keeps the reader thinking.

Activity for your class:

1. Invite students to read the piece silently or aloud.

2. Using highlighters, find and color these:

    *   green—book

    *   yellow—movie

    *   blue—personal experience

3. Circle the truism at the beginning and the "I wonder…" question at the end.

Challenge for students:

Using Ale's pattern, explore your own truism. You can use the text structure below or substitute different types of connections to illustrate your truism, such as a moment from history, the lyrics from a song, or a poem.

Recognizing and Illustrating an Important Theme or Truism

Truism	Book connection	Movie connection	Personal experience	I wonder…

Even though the best people may have flaws, it's their perfections you should concentrate on. The best people may have that one flaw that you always notice, and you can bother them about it and possibly lose them as a friend, or you can concentrate on their perfections and make a good friend.

In the book One *Step Ahead*, Detective Wallander knows that Kalle has some imperfections, but instead of bugging him about it he congratulates him for being such a good cop. Even though Wallander doesn't know it until Kalle is dead, Kalle considered Detective Wallander his best friend, and even though Wallander didn't think of Kalle in the same way, it meant a lot to him.

In the movie "Gone in Sixty Seconds," Memphis Raines is an ex-car thief. He gets back into stealing cars because his brother will be killed if he doesn't deliver all the cars he's supposed to. Memphis is willing to put his life on the line to help his brother, who put himself in this predicament. When people watch this movie they don't think of how bad a person Memphis is because he steals cars, they think, "Wow, this is one great guy willing to put his life on the line to deliver enough cars to save his brother, Kip."

Tristan Griffith is a really good friend of mine who I met in Ricardo, Texas. He sometimes took over a conversation and wrote really long essays that when read, would take up the entire class. He also was one of the most kind and determined people I have ever met. I have never forgotten the time when we had a football game and he showed up to play even though he had crushed his toe by dropping a steel tractor part on it. I think I was just about the only other person apart from his family who knew about this because he never once complained. The day before the game he shoved that toe, which was about half the size of his entire foot, inside his cleats and was our starting runner-back. He is just one of those people who you are never bored around, even in some of the most boring conditions, because he finds ways to have fun and make your time worthwhile.

I have always wondered why some people seem to have an urge to find someone's imperfections, and not their perfections. The world would be a much better place if people actually tried to make people feel good about themselves. ☆

57

Analyzing the Rhetorical Effects of Poetic Devices

> **What Writers Do** — Writers may closely analyze the specific poetic devices a poet employs and the effect created by those authorial choices.
>
> **What This Writer Does** — In this thoughtful analysis, Alison explores Edgar Allan Poe's word choices, mood, and meaning in the poem "Annabel Lee."

Activity for your class:

1. Have students read Alison's analysis BEFORE reading the poem "Annabel Lee."

2. As a class, list some things you learn about the poem from Alison's essay (Example: *the title character is dead*).

3. Find examples to highlight the following two things:

   - green: discussions of poetic devices (Example: *repetition of the title, imagery*)

   - yellow: the effect each device has on the reader (e.g., *repetition of the name and use of the final –ee sound create an echo effect; the imagery creates "creepiness"*)

Challenge for students:

Choose a poem you like or lyrics to a song. Try doing what Alison did, using the main points in the structure below to find and analyze poetic devices.

Point-by-Point Text Analysis

What I notice about the title	What I notice about word choices	What I notice about the speaker's attitudes	What I notice that changes	What I think it all means

Part II. Informative/Explanatory

"Annabel Lee" by Edgar Allan Poe

TITLE—The title introduces us to the *sound* of the name, Annabel Lee, which is important for Poe. He repeats her name seven times, and more than half the lines in this poem end with that *ee* sound. It's almost like the name is shouted out in the title, and then echoes through the rest of the poem. She is the center of this poem, but we never learn much about her except that she was young, the narrator's wife, and her name was Annabel Lee. In a way, the sound of her name becomes her, and takes her place. It's a poem about a girl, but also about the memory of her. She hasn't left much behind for him but the sound of a name he keeps repeating. The title, always the first thing we read, is a great place for Poe to tip us off to this theme.

CONNOTATION and DICTION—In the 5th and 6th stanzas Poe uses romantic metaphors that describe his love for her even after her death and how he thinks of her at almost every moment of the day. In the last couplet of the poem, Poe starts with a poetic description of his wife's state; "*In her sepulchre there by the sea,*" but then he translates his poetic diction into plain terms with "*In her tomb by the sea.*" Repetition is used here not only to augment her state of being but also for Poe to translate the poetic diction of the first line to simpler terms in the second line. When doing this Poe clarifies it for the reader because with the diction and poetic and mysterious sense that pretty much just stems from the word *sepulchre* makes the idea seem more far off and just an unreal thought. This is because *sepulchre* is more of an unknown word which has a mysterious connotation to it. However in the second line *sepulchre* is broken down to *tomb* which has a very real and concrete connotation to all of us.

ATTITUDE—It shows love and death. You learn that the narrator is desperately in love and cannot live without her. He blames God, or the angels for being jealous. He says that he will always love her and he will never get over her. He is just waiting to die, so he can be with her. "*And so, all the night-tide, I lay down by the side/ of my darling, my darling, my life and my bride.*" The speaker seems increasingly obsessed and unbalanced as the poem goes on, and this is what it all leads to. He is half-alive and half-dead, sleeping in a tomb by the ocean.

SHIFTS—The voice, attitude and mood shift from happy to sad and angry in about the second stanza when Poe starts to talk about the death of Annabel Lee and the angels taking her away. In lines 34-37 there is a major shift; the poem goes from past tense to present tense. "*For the moon never beams, without bringing me dreams/ of the beautiful Annabel Lee;/ and the stars never rise, but I feel the bright eyes/ of the beautiful Annabel Lee.*" He was telling a story about something that happened long ago, but now he's letting us know what's happening right now. The increasing shifts and imagery in the lines create a creepiness in the poem.

THEME—The poem means that the author is deeply depressed without his true love. The message in the poem is that true love exists but may not always be happy. It relates to life because it shows that everything doesn't go perfect. It shows that life can be hard sometimes but also that it can be beautiful and fun. Readers will be able to relate to this if they have lost a love one. It is understandable that the author is sad. ☆

Analyzing a Movie

What Writers Do — Writers see things, think about them, and then record their thoughts about what they see, often informally at first.

What This Writer Does — Writing in his journal, Justin records his thoughts about a movie he has seen, creating an interesting, informal analysis.

Activity for your class:

1. Read Justin's piece about the movie *The Good, the Bad, and the Ugly.*

2. Ask students to use highlighters to identify the following:
   - pink— facts about the movie
   - yellow—Justin's thoughts or interpretations
   - green—Justin's final observation about life ("*...we all have a reason for doing what we're doing.*")

Challenge for students:

Think of a movie you've seen that really intrigued you. Write about it. When you've finished, use highlighters to show your details and thinking in the same way that you highlighted Justin's piece.

Movie Self-Discussion

A movie I watched	A history connection	What the movie was really about	What the title might mean	What I wonder

Part II. Informative/Explanatory

I watched "The Good, The Bad, and The Ugly" yesterday. It was interesting that the story was weaved into the Civil War. The movie really captured the brutality of the west and the war. In the end "Blondy" and "The Ugly" teamed up and found the hidden gold of 500,000 dollars. Who could even come up with the title of "The Good, The Bad, and The Ugly?" The man named Duco seemed like he had a hard life which led him to be a criminal. His brother left to be a priest while Duco had to take care of his parents when he was 10 or 12 years old. One would have to watch the movie in order to figure out the rest of Duco's past. I think it proves that we all have a reason for doing what we're doing. Maybe Duco was The Ugly because he had an ugly life. ☆

Creating an "All About" Essay

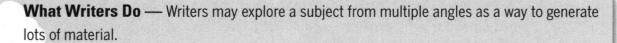

What Writers Do — Writers may explore a subject from multiple angles as a way to generate lots of material.

What This Writer Does — Landri discusses eyes from unexpected angle. The result is a thought-provoking piece that describes her views on the subject.

Activity for your class:

1. Pass out copies of the essay and read the piece with your students.

2. Put students in groups and assign each a different paragraph of the piece.

3. Ask groups to create a list of questions that are answered by their paragraph.

4. Share and discuss.

Challenge for students:

Have each student take a random item from a class collection (e.g., things from students' desks or backpacks; your own collection of tiny toys, candies, or miniatures). Ask them to write responses to the following questions. Allow 2 to 3 minutes for each:

- How would you describe it?
- What can it be used for?
- What is it similar to?
- What is it a part of?
- How can it change?
- What is it the opposite of?
- What can it cause?

Ask students to create a polished essay by deleting or expanding and polishing each response to create an "All About..." essay.

Cubing an Object for an "All About" Essay

Describe it	How it is used	What it is like/unlike	How it can change	What it can cause

The Secret Behind Eyes

The two things most common on your face. They help you see. They're one of your biggest advantages in life. Eyes. I say eyes have more to offer than just being a pretty sight on your face. Sometimes people think they speak louder than words. I believe eyes are the great aspect on someone, the color, shaping, everything it gives you. I learn a lot about a person from their eyes. The sweetness when they blink or the harshness when they stare with a beady look. I also think eyes can be fun, especially for most women and every now and then a guy. There are so many things eyes can be used for. I remember seeing all these mountains driving to Arizona; you couldn't hear that or touch it. Sight to many people is the strongest feature they'll have.

Makeup is my category. I could sit in front of a mirror for hours and hours and just keep redoing my eye makeup again and again. All the different colored eye shadow or mascara even eye liner. I also love putting on the fake lashes. You can have no eye lashes then, boom!! 10 inches of them! Also you have the eye shadow, my absolute favorite. I love trying to look like a famous person or some gorgeous model with my high tech makeup on. Not.

If you're having a bad day or black eye what would you wear to cover it up? Sunglasses! I'm positive I love sunglasses more than anything. I have every kind possible. The different varieties and colors and shapes. I roll with the Oakley's. Yes they're mainly for guys but they do have a girl section stashed in there somewhere. My favorite is the Polarized Oakley Deception. They frame my eyes and go over my eye brows. They're the perfect accessory statement to your face. And protect them from becoming blind.

Now days everyone wants to have colored contacts. Many people who have darker eye color seem to want this color changing. When you're born with brown eyes, be proud of them. You have

them for a reason. Dress them up but not with something that out does them completely. Blue eyes seem gentle. Green eyes seem dangerous. Brown eyes seem confident. Hazel eyes seem to be sweet. Two-toned seem daring. A yellow tint in eyes seems sneaky. Everyone has a different matter in eyes. Some people view the way you move or how you speak. What you drive. Clothes. Shoes. I notice the eyes, as well as many people do. ☆

Giving Writing Vocal Qualities

What Writers Do — Writers sometimes craft a vocal quality in their writing, creating the kind of voice that begs to be read out loud...no...***performed***...for its full effect.

What This Writer Does — Mary Burk fills her witty editorial column with so much voice that a silent reader is almost compelled to read it aloud as she gives lively tips about things to avoid when singing for an audience.

Activity for your class:

1. Distribute copies and ask students to read the piece silently.

2. Invite students to highlight the phrases that they think would sound the best when read out loud.

3. Ask one or more animated readers to perform this piece aloud.

4. Reflect on what parts of the text caused the speaker's voice to animate.

Challenge for students:

Try your hand at writing an advice column like Mary did. See if you can craft a must-be-performed kind of voice. You can use the simple text structure below, if you wish, or another structure of your choice.

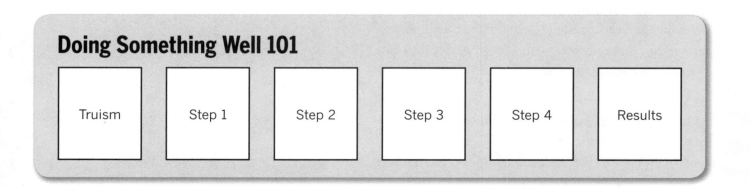

Doing Something Well 101

| Truism | Step 1 | Step 2 | Step 3 | Step 4 | Results |

Success With Singing

If you've ever been to a church service before, it's possible that you've encountered some of the most horrible singing of your life. Now, this is not always so, but in some cases, there's been times where I'd have to get up and 'go to the bathroom' if you know what I'm saying. I saw this happen: Mrs. Cunningham walks up to the mic, and tries to sing *Amazing Grace*. Let's just say, I had to be 'excused' during the performance. Here's some tips on how to *work* the crowd, not *hurt* the crowd.

During her performance, I heard a few things that under *very* few circumstances should you ever do when singing in front of people. Listen and learn.

True or false: the softer you sing, the prettier it sounds; that would be false. You don't have to be *good*, you just have to be *loud*. Mrs. Cunningham tried to sound soft, when really she just sounded like a timid cat hiding behind a tree. So your first tip is to sing loud.

Multiple choice: "Gee maybe I'll sound really _____ if I sing from the back of my throat instead of from my diaphragm." Is it: A.) Good or B.) Bad? The answer is B.) Bad. Newsflash: just because Lady Gaga and Adele can sing like that doesn't mean a human like yourself can. Lady Gaga had voice lessons from a very young age. If you as well have had voice lessons or have been trained to sing from the deep realms of your throat, please knock yourself out, otherwise that brings us to our second tip: Sing from your diaphragm, not the back of your throat. In addition to her *pipsqueak* of a voice, Mrs. Cunningham sang from the back of her throat. Now, she not only sounded like a timid cat, but she sounded like a *dying*, timid cat.

We've now reached our final tip on singing. To give you more of a 'hands-on feel' of what not to do when singing, try singing/saying these words aloud, exactly how they appear: *"Uhhhh-maayyy-singgg guhhh-rayyyceee, how suh-weeet thuhhh sawwnddd, theyaattt sayyyved unnn reyetch like mayyyy."* Really, Mrs. Cunningham? Yes, we know you live in Texas, but could you please not sing the song like a bumpkin? So, lastly, when singing in public, try your very best to put the accent away and just sing the song like how it's originally sung.

Follow these three guidelines, and your next public singing affair should go successfully. So now you know some helpful tips that will hopefully lead you to success with singing! Join me next time for my next article: 'Success With Singing: What Not to Wear When Performing.' ☆

Using Opinions and Facts When Explaining Something New

What Writers Do — Writers anticipate that readers will mentally ask, "How do you know that?" If they want readers to listen, they offer support for their opinions.

What This Writer Does — Sidney describes some pros and cons of allowing kids to use Facebook, thoughtfully offering dangers and benefits for parents to consider. She uses real-life examples and facts to support her thinking, as if she anticipates questions that her readers might have.

Activity for your class:

1. Ask students to imagine what a parent (who doesn't know much about Facebook) might be concerned about when considering whether to let his or her child use this social media site.

2. Pass out copies and read the piece aloud.

3. Look for the author's "answers" in the text. In the margin, have students write a question she might have been anticipating.

4. Decide whether Sidney's statements are facts or opinions; mark F or O next to each.

5. Share responses and discuss the impact of the author's combination of facts and opinions.

Challenge for students:

Think of some part of your world that was not a part of your parents' world and write an essay discussing the pros and cons of it. Imagine the questions they would ask, and answer with your own blend of facts and opinions.

Now Introducing Something

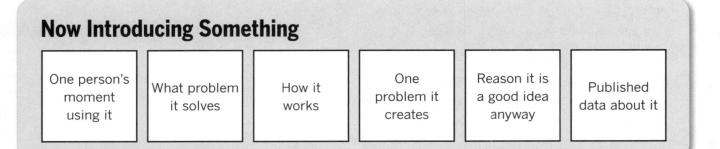

| One person's moment using it | What problem it solves | How it works | One problem it creates | Reason it is a good idea anyway | Published data about it |

Should Kids Have Facebook?

Jill, a forty-year-old mother of 4, always thought her kids were okay to use Facebook. She trusted them and believed that they would only use it to talk to their friends. But one day, she got a call from her 13-year-old daughter's teacher saying that she was called to the office that day for cyber bullying another kid in her class through Facebook. She knew that her daughter had learned her lesson that day, but wondered if she should be allowed to get back on.

Today, kids have found other ways to communicate with their friends besides at school, or occasionally getting to have a play date after a well rehearsed puppy face and much pleading. There has been quite a bit of controversy about whether kids should use the internet to communicate with others, or if it's too risky for cyber bullying. Through Facebook and other connecting sites, the number of depressed kids and suicides have sky rocketed.

I use Facebook, so I understand how addicting it can get. Sometimes it's just the right thing to get you hooked like a new Grey's Anatomy episode, or that irresistible piece of dark chocolate calling your name. You can find old friends you thought you would never see again and meet new ones. You can check up on family members, and follow all of your favorite organizations' pages. As much fun as all of this sounds, kids tend to see it as something else: another way to say something they probably couldn't say in person. You can chat with your online friends, which makes it easy to cyber bully right on the spot.

Some parents don't want their kids to join Facebook because of the "friend" rules. What they don't understand is that you decide who your friends are. You can send anyone you want a request, but if they don't want to be your friend,

you can't change their minds. Also, you can make your page private, so that only your friends can see what you are doing. All in all, if you know how to work Facebook, it can be as safe as you want it to be.

The one problem always goes back to cyber bullying. Lots of times, kids don't understand what their words can do to one person. Some people may have grown up with the saying, "sticks and stones can break my bones but words can never hurt me," but others haven't. Sometimes one more word can make a child decide if they will put up with life one more day, or not. Cyber bullying is a very scary thing, and the more stories kids hear, I think it changes their minds next time they want to say something that isn't very nice.

If you are able to check your kid's Facebook to make sure it is private and trust your kid won't choose to cyber bully, it can be a really good thing. For kids who have recently moved and don't get to see their old friends, or kids who go to camp in the summer with people from out of town, it can be a great way to stay in touch.

According to the National Crime Prevention Center, over 40% of all teenagers with internet access have reported being bullied online during the past year. But with over 400 million users in 2012, Facebook is a choice that offers clear benefits. So like everything else, parents must decide when the time is right for their children and watch over them with wisdom and guidance. ☆

Defining an Important Concept

What Writers Do — When defining an important concept, writers may move from a general truism to specific examples that reveal a deeper understanding of the word.

What This Writer Does — In his opening paragraph, Adrian uses a series of powerful sentence structures that lead the reader to follow his train of thought. At the end of the paragraph, he masterfully moves from a general thought to a specific moment.

Activity for your class:

1. BEFORE passing out copies, ask students to identify the key concept in a typical prompt (Example: *the word "friendship" in the prompt "Write about the importance of friendship."*)

2. Display the following or give it to students on slips of paper. Ask them to fill in the blanks using the above key concept as the first word:

    _____ (*key word from the prompt*) is _____.

    It can be _____ or it can be _____.

    What we don't realize is _____.

    Regardless of what we think about it, _____.

    That's exactly what I saw when _____ (*memory*).

3. Share paragraphs.

4. NOW distribute copies of Adrian's essay and ask a student to read aloud the opening paragraph. Notice how effectively he uses the above structure.

5. Ask another student to finish reading the piece aloud. Discuss how the author's final paragraph circles back to his opening words about choices— and adds to it.

Challenge for students:

Choose a concept like loyalty or bravery. See if you can use a structure like this to move from a general definition to a moment that illustrates its deeper meaning.

Defining the Meaning of a Concept

General meaning of the word	A moment from my life illustrating the word	What that moment taught me about the word	My own deeper meaning of the word

Choices are selections we make every day. They can be choosing what to wear in the morning, what to eat, what music to listen to, or even choosing to pay attention in class. What we don't realize though is that the smallest of choices can affect our whole future. The choices we make in school, at home, and in society can determine what kind of person we become in life and in society. Regardless of what we think about them, our choices can and will affect us for the rest of our lives. Just as my choice to be a pallbearer at my grandmother's funeral affected me and my life.

When I was ten, my grandmother died on New Year's Day. When it came closer to the funeral, my mother approached me with both tears and emptiness in her eyes. She asked me if I would be willing to be a pallbearer at her funeral. I didn't know how to respond. I felt lost and empty inside and as if my feet were made of lead. I didn't know if I was strong enough to accept the fact that I would be the one to put my grandmother in her final resting place. Then I thought to myself, "What would she want me to do?" I searched the desolation deep inside myself and found my strength and an answer. I told my mom that I would do it.

Now that I look back on my choice, I realize how much it meant to not only me, but my family and my grandmother. I think it gave them all strength to see myself, a ten year old boy, carrying his grandmother's casket to her resting place. It showed them that even though I was in a state of despair, I had made a choice to find the strength inside myself and the choice to carry my grandmother's casket. I think that it also made my grandmother happy and proud to see how strong I was even in the state I was in. It made me stronger and gave me hope for the times I would go through in the future.

Choices don't just determine the food we eat or the clothes that we wear. They determine who we are as a person. They determine both our morals and our future. That's what makes choices a true gift. ☆

Writing an Epistolary Essay

What Writers Do — Writers may use letters to tell stories and to illustrate points they want to make.

What This Writer Does — Justin writes an *epistolary essay* (an essay in the form of letters) to make a point about how people can make a difference to the lives of others. He illustrates his point by writing letters between two historical characters, one who is making a historic change and one who is affected by that change.

Activity for your class:

1. Pass out copies of the piece and have two students read the letters aloud to the class.

2. Ask students to identify and highlight what they consider the most important sentence in each letter.

3. Share and discuss responses (answers may vary).

4. Discuss with the class why the writer might have chosen an epistolary format to prove his point. Ask: How would the piece be different if it contained only a speech from Abraham Lincoln, without the personal connection of the second letter?

Challenge for students:

Think about a moment in history, or during your lifetime, when a dramatic change occurred. Write a pair of letters similar to Justin's that explain the change and its impact.

Change Proclamation in Epistolary Form

Letter proclaiming a change	Why the change is needed	How the change will help	Letter of response from someone affected by the change

Fellow Americans,

I, President Abraham Lincoln, Leader of the Union, hereby ensure the freedom of all men, women, and children (regardless of color) under the Government of the Union. Anyone claiming to own a man as property will be arrested and prosecuted. During the duration of these terrible times we must stand together as one whole. For the time of white and black has been abolished! From this era a new Government will arise. A time where we will fight side by side. A time where we will live in peace and harmony as brothers. These desperate times have tried us all. I salute those who have bravely died for our country and bless those people who mourn for them. But as long as there is slavery instated in this land, what we are fighting for will become a meaningless dream. A memory of that one Great land of America, where freedom comes as common as air. Where opportunity was not only for the well and righteous but for all who desire it. For that dream I plead with you join with me and remove our bad deed. Let us abolish slavery once and for all. As a great man spoke these powerful words, so shall I: "united we stand apart we fall."

Sincerely,

A Lincoln

Mr. President,

Dear kind sir. I would like to tell you how grateful I am for you putting a stop to slavery. I can now live a fulfilled life, get married, and watch my children grow just as any other man. I have established my family and am fighting under General Grant. We have never lost a battle and fight with a position of true cause. Every single regiment knows that they are fighting for a true cause. You can see the courage they get after winning a battle. Their enthusiasm carries them further than any other army in the world. We believe in you, Thank you. ☆

Commander Ronnie James

Moving Between Concrete Details and Abstract Ideas

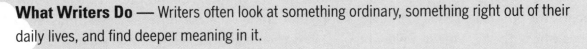

What Writers Do — Writers often look at something ordinary, something right out of their daily lives, and find deeper meaning in it.

What This Writer Does — Elisa narrates the simple task of eating a peanut butter and jelly sandwich. But she finds and articulates profound meaning in the sandwich.

Activity for your class:

1. Read the piece together with your students.

2. Have students reread it with a small group or partner, looking for concrete details versus abstract meaning. Color-code as follows:
   - blue—concrete details (for example, enriched with vitamins, easy-spread)
   - yellow—abstract ideas (for example, one with the bread, unearthly perfection)

3. Discuss the patterns that students find.

Challenge for students:

Think about an object from your daily life. Write an essay about discovering its deeper meaning the way that Elisa did.

The Importance of Something

Its physical properties	What it means to me	What I did	What I discovered

There it sat before me. The most wonderful creation known to mankind. So simple, yet so complex. Everything was in its place, and the entire ordeal was utter perfection. The world was in perfect harmony. There, on the table, was the **perfect** peanut butter and jelly sandwich.

The Iron Kids bread was flawless, enriched with vitamins needed for growing kids and endowed with the shape of a perfect loaf, sliced with precision. Of course, the Welch's Grape Jelly didn't taste like grapes. But it was the best grape jelly **ever**. It was "easy-spread," so the flavor was all over, and it didn't soak into the bread so much that it was nasty, but just enough so that the jelly was one with the bread. Then, the third element: the peanut butter. The smooth Peter Pan brand peanut butter was just the icing on the cake. It was spread evenly on the plane of bread, and when it met the jelly, it was a union made in heaven. This wondrous concoction was the epitome of all good things in the world.

I picked up the sandwich and gazed in awe of its unearthly perfection. Slowly, I raised the sandwich to my mouth and took a bite. I was lost in a state of euphoria. The explosion of taste in my mouth took me back to childhood with memories of Teenage Mutant Ninja Turtles and chocolate pudding. It was as if there was a party in my mouth and only good old PB and J were invited.

I sat there, masticating this delectable morsel and savoring every single ounce of its flavor. Suddenly, it dawned on me. This experience, this state of constant euphoria, is the meaning of life. I stared curiously at the half-eaten sandwich with wonder.

This sandwich of joy had shown me the reason for my being. The reason why we are here is to experience happiness and pleasure. Who knew that all of the answers were here, sandwiched between two slices of bread?

I finished my sandwich and washed my dishes. I haven't shared this information with anyone; however, to this day, my pantry is stocked with peanut butter, jelly, and the key to happiness. ☆

Using Quotations to Support a Thesis in a Literary Essay

What Writers Do — When writers discuss a literary work, they track their thinking, using direct quotations to highlight specific parts of the book or work that influenced that thinking.

What This Writer Does — Selena discusses one of the characters in *Animal Farm* by George Orwell, exploring her belief that this character is an archetype. As she does this, she presents quotations from the book and explains what each quotation reveals about the character.

Activity for your class:

1. Pass out copies and read the piece.

2. Invite students to use highlighters to find the following:
   - blue—the quotations from the book
   - yellow—Selena's analysis of each quotation (what it shows)

3. Look at the pattern, share, and reflect: Does Selena make her thinking clear? Can you think of other ways to explain the material in the quotes?

Challenge for students:

Think of an interesting character from something you've read. If you were to describe that character with one word (or short phrase), what would it be? Just as Selena did, explain what the character did or said in the story, using quotations and explanations to reveal what those quotations show us. Color-code it the same way you did Selena's. What do you see?

Describing a Character

This character is (description)	One way we know (with quotes and explanations)	Another way we know (with quotes and explanations)	These all add up to show us this

Squealer as the Trickster Archetype in *Animal Farm*

In *Animal Farm* by George Orwell, Squealer is a typical trickster archetype. In the novel a farm is taken over by its overworked, mistreated animals. The animals set out to form a utopia of progress, justice, and equality. Through Squealer's archetype of the trickster, Orwell shows that manipulation can be used for power and control.

Squealer fits every attribute of a trickster. Squealer was such a brilliant talker that the others declared that "*he could turn black into white.*" This example shows that Squealer can make you believe what he wants you to believe. He then goes on and tells the other animals that, "*It is for your sake that we drink that milk and eat those apples.*" This shows that he makes the others believe that he cares for them. Both of these examples prove that Squealer is a trickster. He feels so smart that he can control what the others think and do.

Squealer's character fits the theme that manipulation can be used for power and control. When talking to the other animals, Squealer states that Comrade Napoleon, "*would be only too happy to let you make your own decisions for yourselves. But sometimes you might make the wrong decisions, comrades, and then where should we be?*" This example shows that Squealer manipulates the others into thinking that he knows best. He then goes on and states "*Surely, comrades, you do not want Jones back?*" This shows that he appeals to the animals gut instincts and prejudices. He justifies decisions by telling them that the pigs want to break the way of Jones. Both examples prove that Squealer manipulates the other animals into believing that they are making the decisions when it's truly the pigs.

Squealer is so selfish and power-hungry that he is willing to bend reality to suit his interests. He gets what he wants through coaxing and treachery. Squealer does this through exploitation which can be used to bully and demean others, a classic characteristic of the trickster archetype. ☆

Writing an Extended Apostrophe

What Writers Do — Writers discuss their thoughts using various points of view and various levels of formality.

What This Writer Does — Steve discusses his thoughts about death. But instead of the typical third-person, present-tense explanation, Steve addresses death directly, as though death is a person (personification). This rhetorical device is known as an apostrophe; the second-person point of view fits it perfectly into a letter form.

Activity for your class:

1. Pass out copies and read the piece.

2. Ask students to circle the subjects and verbs of each sentence (for example, *Your icy presence is…you appear…you wait…society hates…*).

3. Ask them to highlight the pronoun *you.*

4. As a class, reread portions aloud, converting them into third person (*substituting the words "death" or "it" for each "you"*).

5. Ask students to explain the difference this makes in the effect of the writing. Discuss how personification and point of view have an impact on an audience.

Challenge for students:

Choose an abstract concept (fear, anger, loneliness, guilt) and write to the concept, telling it directly about itself, the way that Steve does. Try using the text structure below.

Directly Addressing a Dreaded Concept

How most people see you	How I see the opposite	How people resist you	How much we actually need you	My words of encouragement to you

      Part II. Informative/Explanatory

Steve Carson
1111 East Pearce St.
San Antonio, TX

May 15, 2012

Death
1234 Right Around The Corner
Earth

Dear Death,

    In the still of the night, your icy presence is felt. Sending chills down the spine of humanity, you appear to kidnap our loved ones without return, never disclosing where they are going. With your cold breath, menacing demeanor, and abnormally dark shadow, you wait until the time is right, strike from the darkness with lightning speed and surgical precision, claiming the consciousness of man. It is for this reason that society hates you. We look at you and all we think of is disgust. I am writing to you to tell you how important I think you are, and that I don't hate you, even though you will bring me sorrow in the future.

    Man fights a timeless war against you everyday. They cannot win, and they will feel the magnanimous tenacity of your clutches sooner or later. It is you that serves the most important role in society. While most people see your actions to be the end of everything mortal, I believe you deserve to be viewed from a different perspective. As life ages and reaches its time in the mortal world, it becomes prone to inevitable expiration (your loving embrace). While its unavoidable demise brings about the end of its mortality, it is the catalyst for being awoken to life in a realm beyond the logically comprehensible. So you are not just a ruthless assassin. You are not just a lunatic hell-bent on expunging all of mankind. Your purpose is oh so vital, and we can't live without you.

    I am writing to you to tell you that we need you, not only to carry out the scheduled appointment you have with everyone, although some try to cheat you and prolong it, but to relieve us of a lifetime of stress. I know that your job is difficult at times, and everyone hates you, but just stay focused, stay positive, and remember that man could not exist without your perpetual kindness. ☆

Sincerely,

Steve Carson

Multimedia Analysis of a Literary Theme

What Writers Do — Writers sometimes get inspired by what they read; a response to a work may be expressed in one or in multiple mediums.

What This Writer Does — After reading *Of Mice and Men* by John Steinbeck, Annie considers one of the novel's themes. First, she writes a poem, using both her own words and words from the novel. She then paints an illustration illuminating the theme. Finally, she writes an explanation of her thinking as expressed in her poem.

Activity for your class:

1. Read the poem aloud, slowly.

2. Discuss, as a class, everything you notice about the patterns in the poem.

3. Notice that the italicized parts are from the novel *Of Mice and Men*.

4. Look at the artwork by the same student.

5. Speculate about why the writer chose the words she did in the poem, what she was trying to convey.

6. Finally, read her explanation.

Challenge for students:

Choose something that you've read, something thought provoking. Choose a theme from that work. Write a poem and/or paint an illustration exploring that theme. Then write an explanation of your poem or painting.

Multimedia Literary Analysis of a Theme

A theme from the literature	A poem, showing the theme (with quotes)	A drawing or painting, illustrating your interpretation of that theme in the literature	My explanation: how I constructed the poem or painting just as I did; how I made choices and what I think they show

Of Mice and Men Poem

to be innocent
      is to be free of burden.
      but we can not choose our burden,
          it is put on us.
          stacks of woe
               are heavy, but joy,
               lightens the load.
                    sorrow and sin reverse the help.
                    All of Lennie's woe came back on him.

to be innocent
      is to not have to be strong.
      but strength is relative,
          and looks deceive those
          who see only weak and strong.
               strength can crush
               those that are weak.
                    "Why he's dead," she cried.
                    "He was so little."

to be innocent
      is to have shelter
      and protection from the winds
          that whisper the secrets of man.
          it is to listen, but not hear,
               to learn, but not know.
               knowledge can break you.
                    As quickly as it had come, the wind died, and the
                    clearing was quiet again.

but along
      this ancient wind we drift,
      learning the secrets
          that will break us,
          and make us strong.
               we have no choice,
               it is our path
               and burden.
                    They had walked in single file down the path, and even
                    in the open one stayed behind the other.

Of Mice and Men Artwork

Of Mice and Men **Explanation**

"Innocence is determined by fate, not choice."

The first quote, *"All of Lennie's woe came back on him,"* was chosen because it showed the way pain is thrown on to victims of suffering, and the helplessness Lennie feels as his innocence is lost and his burdens are gained. He has no choice in these matters, they simply happen to him.

The second quote, *"Why he's dead," she cried. "He was so little."* refers to the puppy that Lennie kills, smothered by too much love and strength. Lennie's physical strength crushes the puppy, but emotionally Lennie is very weak, and he falls prey to those who feel stronger than him.

The third quote, *"As quickly as it had come, the wind died, and the clearing was quiet again,"* came from the end of the book when George is close to shooting Lennie. I used the wind to represent knowledge of the truth, and the way that George shields Lennie from his true fate, so that Lennie can be blissful in his ignorance.

The last quote, *They had walked in single file down the path, and even in the open one stayed behind the other."* used another symbol, the path, to show the way our lives are determined by fate. It also refers to the need for companionship on our paths.

The quotes I used were not chronological from the book, but rather in order of the way I wanted my theme to come across. I used the first to introduce suffering, then the second to address the relativity of strength. The third and fourth were conclusive about my ideas of the way innocence and life are determined by unchangeable forces, represented by the wind or the road.

The part of the poem that was my original writing used key words like "burden," "innocent," and "crush" to show the suffering and gravity of the human condition, and the way our trials pile up on us. ☆

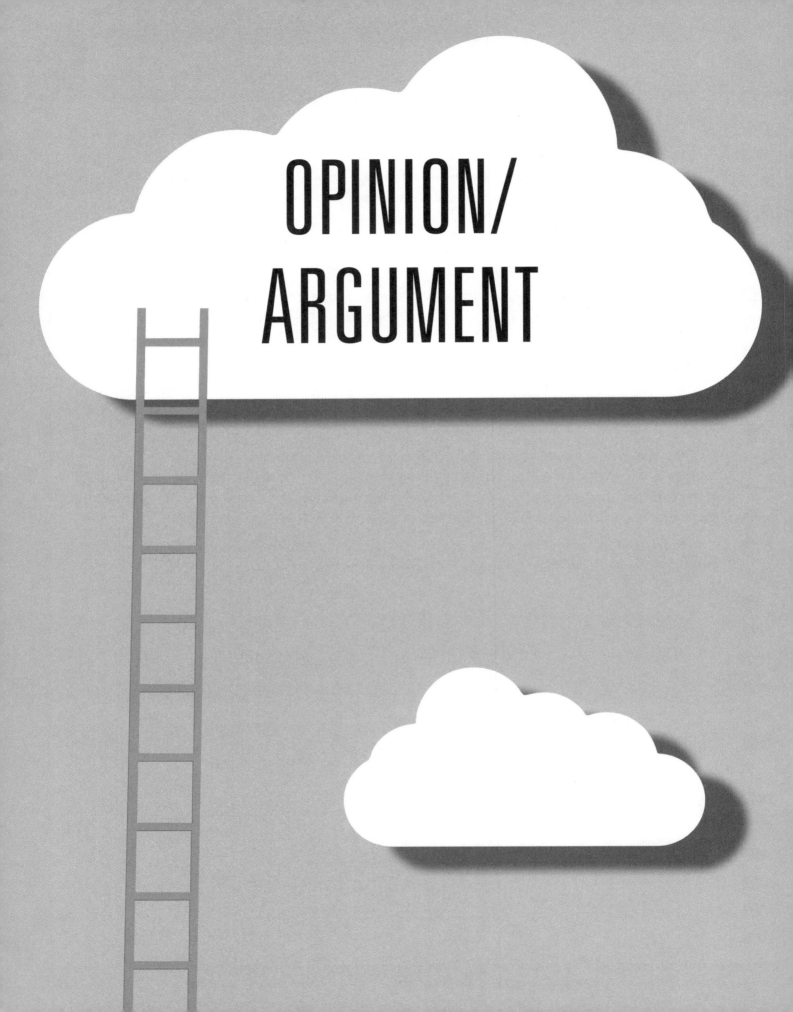

OPINION/
ARGUMENT

A Note About Opinion/Argument

Any time a writer is putting forth a thought, defending a truth, or laying out an opinion, she is creating an argument. The test we used to determine whether a piece belonged in this section is this question: Might a reader or another speaker offer a different thought, truth, or opinion?

Because some of the pieces we have included in this section seem mostly descriptive, they might just as easily have been included in the Informative/Explanatory Writing section. In tests, the lines between the types of writing are rigid and artificially clear. In real life, though, sometimes a piece doesn't fit into a category so neatly.

We advise anyone preparing students for a large-scale writing assessment to study closely the models offered by the assessment source to determine the specific quirks of that assessment instrument. But in a classroom setting, for quality writing instruction, students should learn and practice writing for the many different situations that might require an argument, ranging from opinion pieces to calls to action, debates, literary analyses, and persuasive letters.

The three pieces used in the first three lessons in this section are all written by the same student, Meredith Yoxall. She passionately addresses the problem of homelessness in three different genres: letter, blog, and public service announcement. Nearly any prompt or subject can similarly be addressed in multiple genres.

Using Facts as Evidence

What Writers Do — Writers build convincing arguments by asserting their opinions about a topic and then backing the opinions up with facts.

What This Writer Does — Meredith presents a powerful argument that while there are good programs in place to help the homeless, one segment of the population is being missed. In her letter, she carefully supports her opinions by following them with detailed information and facts. (See the next two lessons for two other formats Meredith used to explore the same topic.)

Activity for your class:

1. Read the letter aloud with the whole class.

2. Individually or in pairs, have students highlight the passages in their copy of the letter as follows:
   - yellow—opinions
   - blue—facts

3. Bring the class back together to compare and discuss results.

4. Share conclusions about the effectiveness of using facts as evidence.

Challenge for students:

Reread an argument you have written or begin a new one. Highlight your facts and opinions in blue and yellow. Find places where your opinions could be strengthened with facts and revise. You may need to consult some outside sources in order to gather needed facts.

As the text structure below shows, Meredith begins her letter by complimenting her audience before stating her argument. Try this yourself sometime.

Politely Asking for Change

| I notice you do this well | I wish you'd also do this | Evidence that the change is needed | Problems I know you'll face | Why it's still worth it |

113 Birdsall Ave.
San Antonio, TX 78155

3/28/11

The National Coalition for the Homeless
2201 P St. NW
Washington, D.C. 20037

Dear National Coalition for the Homeless,

You work on getting homes for small children and the elderly, when 50,000 adolescents in the United States sleep on the streets for six months or more. I am very concerned about the growing population of the homeless. I love that you are helping, but I think you need to do more to help. Between those children and elderly are helpless adults in need.

Some ways to help more would be by questioning the current homeless shelters. Most homeless people don't go to those shelters because of the strict rules. Of course they would not abandon their children. Some homeless shelters will not let families in if they have more than three children. The average length of stay in homeless shelters is 69 days for homeless men, 51 days for single women, and 71 days for families. Some shelters also do not have enough food and beds for everyone.

I think you should take a look at all of those shelters. Pick out the most picky and help them change. We have too many homeless people in the world. Of course this operation would take a long time and a lot of commitment, considering that the average number of shelters for cities with a population of 100,000 is a very high 182. But just imagine the looks on all those faces when you save them. I think a lot of people working together on this will make a big difference in the homeless population numbers. We can go far if we dream big, and once we reach the stars, we go for the moon. ☆

Sincerely yours,

Meredith Yoxall

Using Formal Versus Informal Language

> **What Writers Do** — Writers adjust the formality of their language (register) when they write in different genres or for a different audience. For a formal letter, they use one kind of language; for something informal, like a blog, they make different language choices.
>
> **What This Writer Does** — Meredith shifts to a more conversational, less formal register when she explores the same topic, homelessness, in a blog in the following example.

Activity for your class:

1. Ask a volunteer to read aloud.

2. Pass out copies, and ask students to point out words and phrases that sound more like conversation between friends than formal language that would be used in more professional situations (*Hello...What if I told you...I think...*).

3. Compare the language in this blog to Meredith's formal letter in the previous lesson. Make a t-chart with the headings "Formal" and "Informal." Record examples as students share. Ask, "How would you describe the difference?"

Challenge for students:

Find your most formal piece of writing (or use the text structure below to write a new one about a social problem) and rewrite a little of it as if you are talking to a friend. Notice how your language choices change.

Drumming Up Support

Problem	Why we should face it	What we must do

Part III. Opinion/Argument

March 20, 2011: Homelessness

Hello fellow bloggers! Today I would like to bring forth a very sad topic of interest: homelessness. It is a big conflict and problem in this world. Over 5 million people go homeless each year. Sure, you see homeless people on corners, but they are adults. What if I told you that one out of every three children under 18 are homeless? I think that this is an issue we don't want to face, but if we don't face it now, we will have to face it when it is huge. In the early 1900's, homelessness was not a huge problem, but it started getting worse in the 1960's. I think it is a huge problem already, but many people disagree. As a queen once said, "If they can't afford bread, why don't they eat cake?" And the recession will force 1.5 million more people into homelessness over the next two years. I don't think we can afford to take that chance. We need to get more jobs and fast. But to do that, we will need help. Shelters must become less strict, and we all have to help out. Then, but only then, we can save the homeless. ☆

Writing a Script for a Public Service Announcement

What Writers Do — Writers can choose a variety of formats in which to make an argument, depending on what the situation calls for. A script is an unusual but effective choice.

What This Writer Does — Meredith presents her position about homelessness in several different ways (see the two previous lessons). Here, she presents a lively public service announcement, using the conventions of a script and dialogue to convey her information and argument.

Activity for your class:

1. Assign parts and perform Meredith's public service announcement script. (*Point out the conventions: Action is in parentheses, speech is identified by speaker and colon.*)

2. Discuss the pros and cons of using this format compared to a formal essay or blog.

Challenge for students:

Write a script and film your own public service announcement. Embed your argument in a conversation between characters. End with a persuasive point. You can refer to the text structure below if you need help organizing your information.

Public Service Announcement Script

Establish setting	Conversation interrupted by a sudden problem	Speakers react differently	Conclusion: give imperative "call to action" to readers

Public Service Announcement

Intro: This scene takes place on an urban New York street. Two friends (Avery and Maddie) are taking their daily stroll down the street. It is in modern time, and the friends are walking when confronted by homeless people (Paige, Ally, and Helen) and faced with a choice.

Avery: The party was wonderful last night wasn't it? I really enjoyed the punch but......ugh. Look at those filthy creatures on the corner. People like that shouldn't be alive.

Paige: Excuse me? They have no home. Where are they supposed to go?

Avery: Just walk right past them, those filthy hobos. Actually, we should make some snarky comment that will hurt their feelings. Something like, When's the last time you washed that ugly robe? Or knock over their bag of trash.

Maddie: I can't believe you would say that about innocent people just like we are. Except, you seem to be not so innocent anymore.

All: (turn corner towards homeless people)

Maddie: (puts arm around Helen) Come home with me, I'll help. (leads Helen away)

Helen: (Grabs bag and shuffles off with Maddie)

Avery: Fine, maybe I'll be nice. Here. (hands $4.00 to Ally) Go buy yourself a low fat Mocha.

Paige: (skips off camera screen)

Narrator: Don't just have a life. Save a life." ☆

Examining Quotations

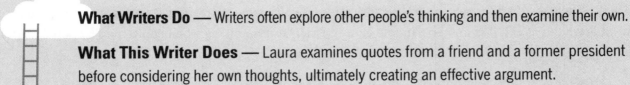

What Writers Do — Writers often explore other people's thinking and then examine their own.

What This Writer Does — Laura examines quotes from a friend and a former president before considering her own thoughts, ultimately creating an effective argument.

Activity for your class:

1. Distribute copies and read the piece with students.

2. Together, look at the text structure below.

3. Ask students to find where these chunks of text start and stop in Laura's essay. Circle the chunks.

4. Have them highlight the opening sentence in each chunk. Ask for volunteers to read their highlighted sentences aloud to hear Laura's "kernel essay."

Challenge for students:

Find a quotation you especially like. Try out this text structure to help you with a discussion of that quotation. Write one sentence for each box to create a kernel essay. Add in details the way Laura did for a complete essay.

Comparing Notes

Some people think...	And other people think...	But I think...	What that tells me

Versions of Quiet

Some people say little because they aren't social, or maybe they just don't take an interest in the conversation. A good example of this was when I was talking to Chris. I was voicing my opinions about politics and I was getting fired up as usual! I noticed that Chris wasn't responding. I stopped mid sentence and asked him what was wrong. He stared at me blankly for a second, then replied. "Well, I'm not much of a talker and I don't know much about politics anyways…" Some people don't talk because they really don't have anything to say, or they're just antisocial. I decided to add this thought to my mental database.

Other people say little because they don't want to start an argument. Another reason Chris wouldn't talk was due to the fact that he was secretly of the opposing political party. He was very into politics, but he didn't want to voice his opinions and cause a rift in our friendship. He knew discussing politics would spark a large argument and "cause a fire-storm." By nature, Chris is a neutral type of guy and he detests debates. I guess it was a good reason for him to keep his mouth shut. I added this thought to my database: some people keep quiet to avoid conflict, confrontation and so on.

Finally, I ask myself; why do I speak little? I pondered long and hard, I formed a hypothesis and set up algebraic equations. After all this I realized the "solution" was simple. I just don't particularly like talking. But when I do talk I make sure it's something of importance. This gives me an advantage! When I do speak people turn their heads to hear what the quiet girl is going to say. Another important thing I make sure to do is *"Be sincere; Be brief; Be seated."*—Franklin Delano Roosevelt. This is one of the most important things to keep in mind when speaking. Just get to the point and everything else will fall into place.

This tells me that words can be a powerful tool, and they should be kept to a minimum. All of this makes sense now, thanks to Franklin Delano Roosevelt's quote *"Be sincere; Be brief; Be seated."* You don't have to tell a story to get your point across. Maybe we can finally get those chatterboxes to minimize their words. ☆

Developing Sentence Variety

What Writers Do — Writers use a variety of sentence types, lengths, and structures. This creates rhythm and can make the writing feel conversational rather than robotic.

What This Writer Does — In his essay about a favorite remote-control car, Daniel masterfully uses all four sentence types (declarative, interrogative, imperative, and exclamatory), two points of view (first and second person), and all four sentence constructions (simple, compound, complex, and compound-complex).

Activity for your class:

1. Pass out the piece and read it aloud or choose a student volunteer.
2. Together with students, search for and label different kinds of sentences (Interrogative—*Do you have a favorite...?* Imperative—*Grab a remote.* Simple—*It's my remote control car.* Compound-complex—*I can recall a time...* Second person—*Why spend all your money?*).

Challenge for students:

Let's imitate one of Daniel's sentences. Look at the sentence construction in the last sentence of his second paragraph. See how it fits the following pattern:

If it does this or this, you can do this and then this, and this will happen.

Using the sentence template below, fill in the blanks with new content, creating as many different sentences as you can.

If it does _____ or _____, you can _____ or _____, and _____ will happen.

Try placing your surprising new sentences in a piece of your own. You can use the text structure below if you wish.

Traditional 5-Paragraph Essay Minus One

Opinion because of A and B	How I know A	How I know B	Opinion intensified, renamed

---

Do you have a favorite toy, game, or doll? I do. It's my remote control car. It's called a Cyclaws. They call it Cyclaws because if it gets stuck in the grass or anything that's hard to get to, it charges fast and uses regular wheels and claws. Grab a remote to a car and come see why Cyclaws are the best.

To begin with, Cyclaws are awsome because they never get stuck. They use special wheels that turn into a claw when they are stuck. They can go through mud, dirt, even grass and hills. That is so cool. I can recall a time when my Cyclaws was going on a muddy hill that was really steep. It only took 5 seconds to get up. And also if it gets stuck or flips upside down, you can go in reverse really fast, then suddenly go forward and it will flip right-side up.

In addition to never getting stuck, Cyclaws is the bomb because it charges fast. It only takes about 40 seconds to charge! After the 40 seconds are over, it can go around the Earth 1,000,000,000 times! I remember it went about 70 M.P.H. (Miles per hour). I could win a race with this thing! It is as fast as a mustang. No! It's a jet plane! Why spend all your money on some tattered old car, when you can buy a Cyclaws. It's the best toy I have ever owned!

In conclusion, Cyclaws is the best because it never gets stuck. And best of all, it charges in 40 seconds. I wish I was at home playing with my Cyclaws. I hope school is over. Cyclaws is a boy's best friend. ☆

Using Personal Experiences to Support Opinions

What Writers Do — Writers often back up opinions (also called claims or assertions) by sharing personal experiences to illustrate their points.

What This Writer Does — Arianna expertly weaves a specific, focused memory into each of three different points she makes to illustrate why she loves Saturdays: She can be lazy, she can go fishing with her dad, and the family has special dinners.

Activity for your class:

1. Distribute copies of Arianna's essay and have students read the piece.

2. Ask students to use highlighters to find and color these items:
   - yellow—opinions
   - green—the author's memories and experiences

3. Reread the piece aloud, omitting all of the green parts, to hear a less effective version of this piece. Discuss: What are the differences?

Challenge for students:

Look at one of your own opinion pieces and highlight it the same manner. In this way, you can see if you have used personal experiences as evidence for an opinion. If you don't have any, try adding in some short anecdotes to see how that works as a tool for strengthening your piece.

Traditional 5-Paragraph Essay

Opinion because of A, B, C	How I know A	How I know B	How I know C	Restate opinion

"Hurray!" I shouted as I exploded with laughter. It was Saturday, my favorite day of the whole week.

Saturday is my kind of day because I get to sit around and be as lazy as a big, huge, fat, cat, I get to go fishing with my dad, and for dinner, we have a buffet.

"Initiating lazy cat countdown. 5, 4, 3, 2, 1! You may begin being lazy." This is the first thing I do on my Saturday. When I say I am lazy I really mean it because all I do when I'm lazy is sit on the couch and watch T.V.

I remember one crisp Saturday in November, I was too lazy to get out of bed and the sun was shining brightly on my face so I pulled the covers over my whole body. My family was wondering where I was and they searched for me for hours and right when they were about to call the police, they looked under my blanket and there I was.

Something else I do on my superb Saturdays is fish with my dad. I love the mushy sea water smell of the beach where my dad and I love to fish. When we feel the damp, but warm sand squish up between our toes, we know that we will have a great time.

I remember one blazing hot Saturday my dad and I were having a great time fishing at the beach. I felt a slight tug on my line and then it got bigger, and bigger, and bigger until before you know it I'm being pulled along in the water by a fish. My dad ran in to get me before I was pulled out to sea. That was a Saturday I won't forget.

Get ready to fill your plates at my house because every single Saturday we have a huge buffet. We usually have a scrumcious chicken with steaming gravy (and of course we have other food). I remember a chilly Saturday in December when we were enjoying our buffet. I got stuffed so full that I couldn't move and I slept in the kitchen. That Saturday was my absulute favorite of them all. ☆

Using Verbs and Adjectives to Back Up Opinions

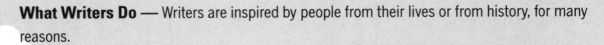

What Writers Do — Writers are inspired by people from their lives or from history, for many reasons.

What This Writer Does — In the following kernel essay, Devyn sets up an argument that Joan of Arc is admirable, using a clear line of thinking to lead to this conclusion. Devyn's verbs identify Joan's actions, while his adjectives reinforce her personality traits.

Activity for your class:

1. Pass out copies and have students read the piece.

2. Ask them to underline the main point (which occurs in both the beginning and ending).

3. Have students use highlighters for the following activities:

    • yellow—circle any words or phrases that show Joan's personality traits (*adjectives*)

    • green—underline any words or phrases that show Joan's actions (*verbs*)

    • blue—highlight the effects of these traits and actions on other people

Challenge for students:

Think about someone from history about whom you have a strong opinion. Write a short piece about that person, explaining your opinion. Make sure to use both the person's traits and actions to back up your opinion. You can use the text structure below to write a kernel essay, which you can then fill out with details.

Opinion Piece About a Historical Figure

Why I chose the person	One quality he or she had	One moment I saw that quality	How that affected the people	My opinion about the person

---

Joan of Arc

In school everyone has a favorite person to study, and everyone likes that person for a certain reason. They might like them because they are jealous of them or maybe that person is just interesting. For me the reason I like my favorite person is because she is a great role model. My favorite person is Joan of Arc.

Joan was a brave and powerful woman. She was also very strong considering she was only 18.

Joan dressed up in boys' clothes, cut her hair, and entered battle. This is when Joan was strong and powerful.

Joan gave hope to the people, their spirits rose when they saw her. Joan gave them a chance of defeating the English.

Joan of Arc should not just be a role model to me, she should be a role model to the whole world. ☆

Making a Claim About a Historical Event

> **What Writers Do** — Writers sometimes make a claim about a historical event, using additional events from history to support their claim.
>
> **What This Writer Does** — Sofia poses the argument that King Henry wasn't to be blamed for the murder of Thomas Beckett; she supports her claim with a description of the events that led to the murder.

Activity for your class:

1. Pass out copies and ask students to read the piece.

2. Direct students to highlight the following:
   - green—actions
   - yellow—phrases involving emotions

3. Discuss the cause-and-effect relationships between these. (Example: *"All because of Henry's anger"* [yellow] caused *"someone got murdered."* [green])

Challenge for students:

Think of an event in history that you think should not have happened. Describe what went so wrong that this event *did* happen. You might want to use the text structure below that Sofia used.

Making a Claim About a Historical Event

Event	Why this happened	When it happened	What people thought then	What I think now

The Murder

All because of Henry's anger, someone got murdered. King Henry was angry because of a law that he wanted to have, but Thomas Beckett did not agree. Henry was talking and said, "Who will get rid of Thomas?" Three knights heard him and went to get Thomas.

The knights got to Thomas. They tried to drag Thomas out, but he said, "Ready to die for my lord," and the knights killed him in the church.

When King Henry found out what happened to his friend he was very upset. The people were very mad with King Henry, but very sad about the death of Thomas Beckett.

I think it was a big mistake because King Henry didn't really mean it. It was really the knights who killed Thomas. ☆

Using Sensory Details

What Writers Do — Writers often use their senses in description to help support their main points.

What This Writer Does — Katie leads off with a great example of onomatopoeia (*Crackle, Crackle*) to describe the sound of fall, and she includes many additional effective sensory details in her essay about why autumn is her favorite season. These details help convey the full flavor of her opinion about that season to her readers.

Activity for your class:

1. Pass out copies of the essay and read the piece together.

2. Have partners or small groups go on a hunt through the piece, looking for sensory details.

3. Circle the examples of things the author sees, hears, smells, feels, and tastes.

4. Label them with sensory icons (using small drawings of eyes, ears, nose, hands, lips).

5. Share and discuss with classmates: How do sensory details add to a piece?

Challenge for students:

Write about your favorite season using the text structure below, or revise a piece you have already written. Try adding more sensory details, labeling them with the same icons.

Why This Season Is My Favorite

Opinion because of A, B, C	How I know A	How I know B	How I know C	Restate opinion

Part III. Opinion/Argument

Crackle Crackle, the sound of fresh fallen leaves. It's fall, I can tell. Fall is my favorite season because I love the leaves and weather. Can't forget Halloween. So grab your rake and I'll tell you why fall is my favorite season.

First of all, fall is my favorite season because I love the leaves. They look like a beautiful butterfly, the leaves as the wings. Also I love to jump into them. When I do that I feel as though I could fly. I remember when I used to live in North Carolina I adored the color changing leaves, but that wasn't my favorite. My favorite was to jump in and make leaf angels, and when I walked into the house I had leaves everywhere.

In addition to the fall leaves, I cherish fall because of the weather. I love the weather because it's just right, not too cold and not too hot. I adore the feeling when you walk in the house and it's all warm and toasty with a slight smell of chocolate cookies in the oven. MMMMMmmmmmmmmmm...Let's get back on track, so the weather in fall is just right to play in, the cool weather.

Last but not least, I think highly of fall because of Halloween. Halloween is AWSOME because of the candy and costumes. I adore dressing up as different people. I remember last year when I was Velma and I was drop dead gorgeous. I looked almost perfect, and I got a ton of candy. WOW! All kinds too!

Now you know why I value fall. I love the leaves and weather. Can't forget Halloween. Fall is perfect. So what's your favorite holiday? ☆

Using Parentheses

What Writers Do — Writers use many different kinds of punctuation for clarity, but they also use it to add style, flavor, and voice.

What This Writer Does — In this essay about her favorite possession, Maryssa's skillful use of parentheses, ellipses (...), exclamation, points, and question marks takes punctuation way beyond mastery and correctness into the realm of style and creativity—and adds to the reader's enjoyment of her piece.

Activity for your class:

1. Read the piece aloud after distributing copies to the class.

2. With a partner, have students highlight all the places where Maryssa used parentheses to enclose a new phrase.

3. Partners discuss: What did theses phrases add to the piece? How did they change it?

4. Ask volunteers to read the sentences aloud with the parenthetical expressions removed. Talk with the class about how the essay would sound different without them.

Challenge for students:

Look at any piece you have written. See if you can work in some parenthetical comments to add new information the way Maryssa did. Then compare the results.

Traditional 5-Paragraph Essay

Opinion because of A, B, C	How I know A	How I know B	How I know C	Restate opinion

Do you know what my favorite possession is? A Sock Monkey! This is my favorite possession because: you can go to school with it, play with it, and sleep with it. I adore my sock monkey.

First of all, this is my favorite possession because you can go to school with him. I remember I had to go to P.E. (phisical education) when I realized I had to change in a uniform in a...LOCKER ROOM! I looked behind me and I viewed sock monkey peeking out my rose red backpack. I pushed open the door and did a nose dive into someone's old wet gym sock. That's when I found my locker and transformed into my volley ball outfit. I'm glad that's over.

Another reason is you can play with him. My favorite time was when Gabriella came over to my house for the hot summer. We would play tea party outside with my Barbies that were posing. (We made the one with the super glued head that was stuck all the way to the neck, Ha Ha, the maid). Then her stuffed unicorn was the photographer and secretly had a crush on my sock monkey. We would play for hours until it was pouring rain out and we had to go inside. But when we did the power would go out. That was the time we would start goofing around with glow sticks and play fairy princess.

Last but not least, you can sleep with him. For example, when Miss Galdoer (my friend) and I would go to sleep, we would shove the glow sticks under the bed so Mom wouldn't find out we used them and we crawled into bed. She and I were facing each other clutching our stuffed animals and snuggling under my night light as we quietly devoured chocolate ice cream with some Hershey syrup drizzled down the side and oozing to the bottom of the bowl. We soon passed out with chocolate mustaches over our mouths. Sock Monkey and I cuddled in the cozy covers and fell into a deep sleep as the sound of rain drops tapping on the window faded away.

So now you know that a Sock Monkey is my favorite possession. Even if you're in a locker room he is still with you. "YUCK! That's a stinky sock!" ☆

Naming and Renaming

What Writers Do — Writers sometimes avoid repeating a key word in a piece by using alternatives to that word—often more descriptive, intriguing substitutes.

What This Writer Does — Savannah expertly renames her Barbie doll in each description of her favorite companion, adding voice, humor, and sparkle to her writing.

Activity for your class:

1. Pass out copies and read this piece together with the class.

2. Ask students to look for the Barbie references and highlight them as you scan through it together. (Example: *Miss Prissy Princess, bodacious Barbie, my little plastic princess, miss know-it-all, the smart alick, my crosseyed plastic figure, my rinkely melted toy*)

3. List the examples on a chart. Ask students to think about using alternatives to a key word like Savannah did. What do these alternative words add to the piece? How do we do the same thing in real life with nicknames?

Challenge for students:

Revisit one of your pieces and find one key word you repeated. Brainstorm a list of alternative words to substitute for that key word and try substituting the alternatives. Read the results aloud to see if you like the changes.

Traditional 5-Paragraph Essay

Opinion because of A, B, C	How I know A	How I know B	How I know C	Restate opinion

What is tan, made of plastic, and has gorgeous blond hair? My favorite possession...Miss Prissy Princess (barbie)! I adore my bodacious barbie because: you can talk to her, dress her up, or you can take her wherever you dream to go! I love barbie!

First of all, I love to talk to my little plastic princess because she always listens to me! One time I think barbie was so interested in my story she didn't blink, she just sat there! I even remember that her eyes were a little crosseyed! She was in a tie-died shirt and a gingham skirt! Every day as I walk home from a long humid day at Lincoln Park elementry I would do my math homework and miss know-it-all or the smart alick would help with home work! Even though she didn't talk it was like she sent me these strange messages in my mind like, "bX = 9 the answer is 3 × 3 = 9!" she would bellow. I love my crosseyed plastic figure!

In addition, I like to dress barbie up! For example I dressed my very first barbie in a plaid dress, striped florescent pink and jet black striped stockings, and a checkered hat! (Tip: The reason Barbie is rinkely is because my little pint-sized sister Miss Buger Picker got into Mom's stuff and blowdryed her and she melted like a candle!) My favorite place to dress her up in is in my tree house. I like to bring a bucket of hot water in my tree house and lay barbie in it with her flamboyant bathing sute on! Then I wrap her in a gargantuan Oak leaf to pretend it's a towel. I love my rinkely melted toy!

Last but not least, I like to bring barbie everywhere I go! One time I brought barbie to school and as I was riding the yellow school bus home I rolled down the window. The next think I know she flew out my backpack and out the window! She swiftly landed on the road with a crash! Then a plum purple Mustang ran her over and her head fell off! The next day me and mom went thrifting and found another doll! I love dolls!

So now you know, that a barbie is my favorite possession! And Btw. (by the way!) don't roll the window down if you have your barbie in your gingham b.p. (back pack!) by-by-barbie! Squash! Oh-no barbie your head! ☆

Using an Innovative Format

What Writers Do — There are many standard formats for persuasive essays, but sometimes writers find innovative ways to present their information.

What This Writer Does — Wyatt converts his argument into a news story that contains news breaks, interview questions, a live toss (the reporters taking turns at the mike), and background information woven into the report. The position and reasons are all visible and compelling.

Activity for your class:

1. Distribute copies and read the news story aloud, having different students take the parts of the newscaster, Wyatt, and Patty.

2. Next, have students find and highlight the components of the argument:
    *   yellow—the thesis statement, the main claim
    *   pink—the three main reasons
    *   blue—the proof presented by the writer for each reason (circle this)

Challenge for students:

Select any persuasive piece that you have created before. Try rewriting it into a newscast similar to this one. Make sure you include all the components of your argument the way Wyatt did. How does your piece sound different even if you use the traditional text structure below?

Traditional 5-Paragraph Essay

Opinion because of A, B, C	How I know A	How I know B	How I know C	Restate opinion

"This just in, we're talking about kids' favorite possession. Lets focus on a kid named Wyatt Gillingham. Now Wyatt you say your prized possession is a skateboard. Why do you like it?" "Well you do awesome tricks, it's vibrant, and it's a challenge." "We'll be right back after the break."

"Your first reason is you can do awesome tricks, am I correct?" "Yes you are," "Can you give us an example?" "For example in my driveway I have the sickest (coolest) ramp ever. We painted it gecko green. My coolest trick is doing a 360° in air and landing it. How many ten year olds can do that? That's a mighty good reason."

"Moving right along, he says his skateboard is very vibrant. Let's check in with pinched faced Patty, "Hello Patty." " Hello Bob." "We are here in Wyatt's back yard and he has a massive halfpipe. We brought our radar gun to test his speed. Wyatt is over here strapping on his pads. Now he has been injured before, right?" "Yes! Once he was out here with no pads on and he landed wrong and broke his elbow. But he is still here today."

"Anyway let's get back with the speed mission. 3...2...1...GO! He is just a pumpin' out here. He's makin' really smooth turns, his nickname is flying tomato because he has strawberry shortcake red hair and he soars like an eagle. The results are in, 15 miles an hour. Wyatt is the speed king!"

"Last it is a challenge. Wyatt, what type of challenges do you face?" "Extreme challenges!" "Like what?" "Well it was a bright sunny day in the small town of Mims when I saw a...twenty step staircase! I knew what I had to do, jump it! About the tenth time I got so much speed that I landed it perfectly. I was so overjoyed I jumped off my board and did a...happy dance!"

"Evidence proves that the skateboard is Wyatt's favorite possession. Wyatt says he will never forget how he soared like an eagle going 15 miles an hour on his mega halfpipe! ZZZOOOOOMMM!! ☆

Using Internal Citations

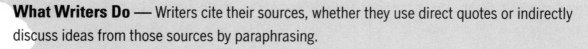

What Writers Do — Writers cite their sources, whether they use direct quotes or indirectly discuss ideas from those sources by paraphrasing.

What This Writer Does — In this essay about the effects of too much homework, Abbie uses both direct quotes and paraphrases, citing the authors of the works she used in parentheses.

Activity for your class:

1. Distribute copies and read the piece with your students.

2. Ask students to highlight all of the parentheses.

3. Ask them to notice where Abbie used quotation marks in the second paragraph. Ask students: What do the quotation marks tell the reader? *(that these are direct quotes from source)*

4. Next, point out how Abbie did *not* use quotation marks near the other highlighted citations. What might this show? *(paraphrased information)*

5. Together, write a class list of "rules for citing sources" based on Abbie's piece.

Challenge for students:

Read several articles about one topic, and then plan and write an essay stating your opinion about the topic. Cite the sources used in your piece the way that Abbie did.

Taking a Stand Against Something

Opinion because of A, B, C	How I know A	How I know B	How I know C	Restate opinion

Did you know that too much homework messes up kids' social lives? Well, it does, including mine. I miss parties, sports, and sleepovers. Not only that, but it makes kids hate school and causes a lot of stress. Education is very important, but developing social skills and belonging to groups outside of school is important too. Too much homework gets in the way of being involved in anything outside of school.

"Piling mountains of homework on children is no doubt the way to turn education into drudgery. And once that happens, curiosity dies and soulless, sullen, mechanistic compliance takes over" (Richard). Do teachers want kids to wake up remembering that they have an hour of homework left to do or wake up remembering that they barely had any homework and they like their teachers even more?

I believe that Wednesdays should be reserved for midweek church or a kid's religion, or just as a break. They could also connect more with their religion or families than just on Sundays or weekends. And for days with homework assignments, it would be a lot easier on the kids and their parents if they just had about 30 to 45 minutes of homework.

A study by professors at the University of Toronto showed that many families, even with children in early grades, struggle with the stress of homework overload. Homework should be over the material covered in class and should take a limited amount of time in case of extracurricular activities and unexpected conflicts with family. Research shows that some second grade students have less than ten minutes a night and some over 45 minutes a night of homework. Second graders can't handle all of that homework! Research also shows that homework makes kids stay up late and most likely not listen to the lesson the day after. Homework also ruins family holidays! Do you want kids on Christmas or New Year's to be doing homework instead of enjoying vacation with their families?

If you are a teacher, think about when you were a kid. If you have kids, think about the things they are doing and what they want to do. Kids are busy. Don't put more stress on them with tons of homework that really isn't necessary. School is important, but having a life is, too. ☆

Editors' Note: Abbie's bibliographic information has been omitted in the publication of this essay, but her internal citations are included in the text of the essay for demonstration purposes.

Drawing Editorial Cartoons

What Writers Do — Writers sometimes make their points through cartoons, conveying their ideas more efficiently through images than through words.

What This Writer Does — Abbie's cartoon goes right to the heart of what parents experience when they see their children struggling to keep up with their homework. She includes lots of key details about the situation through her simple images.

Activity for your class:

1. Give your students copies of the cartoon.

2. Invite them to look at the picture and then lightly circle every part that reveals what she thinks about her topic.

3. Ask students to choose one or two of the places circled and write a sentence explaining Abbie's thinking.

4. Share and discuss.

5. Talk about how these points might be turned into an essay.

Challenge for students:

Choose a persuasive essay you have written (or write a new one using the text structure below) that makes several points about a topic. Try sketching a stick-figure cartoon that makes all of your points, using as few words as possible.

Traditional 5-Paragraph Essay

Opinion because of A, B, C	How I know A	How I know B	How I know C	Restate opinion

Is this your child?

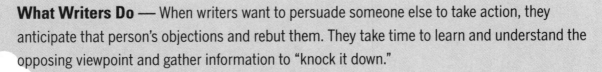

Knocking Down the Opposition

What Writers Do — When writers want to persuade someone else to take action, they anticipate that person's objections and rebut them. They take time to learn and understand the opposing viewpoint and gather information to "knock it down."

What This Writer Does — Avery sets up an argument about animal adoption. In this piece, there are three serious objections by people who resist animal adoptions. The author then refutes each one using information gathered from published sources.

Activity for your class:

1. Invite a volunteer to read the piece aloud after passing out copies.

2. Ask partners or small groups to reread it, looking for objections or opposing points of view. Underline those.

3. Then have students find places where this author dispels the objections and circle those.

4. Talk about which is more effective: stating positive reasons and proof or stating negative points and rebutting them.

Challenge for students:

Look for an argument you have written (or write a new one) in which you try out this idea by writing up objections from the other side and refuting them. Use the text structure below to be sure you cover the main ideas.

Knocking Down the Opposition

Opinion/ argument	1st objection that people have (and why it's wrong)	2nd objection that people have (and why it's wrong)	3rd objection that people have (and why it's wrong)	Restatement and call to action

---

Animal Adoption

Do you own a pet? If more than 57% of U.S. households own pets, why not yours (AKC)? There are many reasons, to be sure, but pets seem to have more benefits than problems when adopted into a home. Not only do pet owners prove this fact, but statistics are right there to back them up.

The main issue with having a pet is allergies. Parents think that if they are allergic to pets, any trace of hair will immediately send them to the doctor with a huge rash. This, as Dr. Gern proudly states, is a common assumption and should not be taken seriously. A growing number of studies have suggested that children growing up in homes with a pet or on a farm where they are exposed to animals are less likely to have serious problems with asthma and allergies. This is mainly because dogs are dirty animals and people with more exposure to that dirt and allergens will build up a stronger immune system (Gern).

You may have heard that pets are just a nuisance for the elderly population of the country. That, as many things seem to be, is incorrect. Studies done on elderly homes and nursing facilities have proved many ways animals help them. Whether it's getting them energized to exercise or raising their self-concept and competence, they seem to do it all (McClasky)

Did you know that only petting a dog could have a serious affect on your attitude? It's true, proved by both doctors—Parello and McConnell. Watching a lassie flick its tail back and forth has shown to lower their levels of cortical (the hormone associated with stress).

Alzheimer's is a growing disease, and is a cause for not wanting a pet. If you have Alzheimer's, depending on what stage you are in, you are constantly forgetting and you have the fear of forgetting to feed the pet or something that could be fatal to your lovely pet. This may be true, but studies by Dr. Beck have shown unbelievable facts. Beck put a bowl of goldfish in the dining room of a nursing home where several patients had Alzheimer's and did not want to eat, therefore losing weight at an unhealthy rate. She found, to her shock, that most of the patients experienced an appetite increase and weight gain. After that experiment, she tried other methods, such as making the light better or screening an old movie— to no avail. It seemed, whatever the reason, only that simple bowl of fish seemed to trigger that (Beck).

What about love connections? Have you ever been over to a friend's house to work on a project and you ended up paying attention to only their pet? Dogs help start a conversation and ease people out of isolation.

Dogs, cats, fish…they're all great pets. Statistics and people both prove that they are not only good for your health, but also for your personality and relationships. So why not get one for yourself?

"A pet is a medication without side effects that has so many benefits." ☆

—Dr. Creagan

Editors' Note: Avery's bibliographic information has been omitted in the publication of this essay, but the internal citations are included in the text of the essay for demonstration purposes.

Using Quirky Mental Images in an Argument

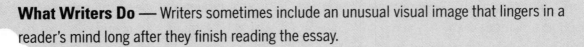

What Writers Do — Writers sometimes include an unusual visual image that lingers in a reader's mind long after they finish reading the essay.

What This Writer Does — In this argument, Lee brings one of those delightful, quirky images into his reasoning about the benefits of sleep. For example, a reader can picture his messed-up hair after too little sleep. And there might be additional images that linger with readers as well.

Activity for your class:

1. Have a volunteer read the piece aloud before passing out copies.

2. Ask, "We know the author's main point is that getting enough sleep is important. But as you think about what we just read, what part of his essay do you remember first? What can you still picture? Jot down answers on sticky notes and then we'll post them on a class chart."

3. Give students copies of the essay now. Together, discuss which answers on the chart are mental images that Lee gave the reader. Put a check mark by all of those.

4. Share and reflect on the value of quirky mental images from the writer to the reader.

Challenge for students:

Try writing an argument describing one of your favorite activities and recommending it to people. Include your experiences with the activity, how it works, and its benefits. Try including some quirky mental images that will stick in the minds of your readers.

Check out the text structure below for ideas.

Why This Is My Favorite Activity

I like to _____	My first experience with it	How you do/play it	How it makes you feel	Positive results

Why I Need Sleep on a School Day

I like to sleep a lot. It is a great thing to get enough. I used to not like sleep because it was boring. Now, I love it. Plus, it beats doing the laundry on Saturday and Sunday. Refreshing sleep is wonderful and is great after an active day.

The first time I got more than enough sleep on a school day, I felt great. I felt refreshed and ready. My tiring self during the day was not I on that day. School is easy on a day when you get enough sleep. It is much easier to pay attention and listen. Also, you don't fall asleep during class. It is very helpful and, I don't know if this is an opinion or fact, but it seems that students do better during the school day when they get a sufficient amount of sleep the night before. Sleep is vital.

To go to sleep, all you have to do is close your unfocused eyes, put a blanket on yourself, and stay silent the entire time in the night before you fall into sleep. I walk to my room; I see the bed and wish I were in it. Then I get in. On cold days, wear a blanket. On hot days, don't wear a blanket. Sometimes you find that perfect position to sleep in and if you stay like that you should have no trouble falling asleep and waking up in the morning.

If you sleep well the entire night, you should wake up with ease and feel refreshed and ready. I abhor being tired. Sleep, the opposite of sports, can turn someone into a very alert person. In the mornings, I make my lunch and my breakfast. I walk downstairs, see my dog, and then I gripe, "I am so tired." But if I get good sleep, I'll make them both easily. You just feel so good when you get enough sleep. And I know there is such a thing as beauty sleep. Because when I get little sleep, I look at my messed up hair in the mirror. But when I get a lot of sleep, I look perfectly fine.

When you get enough sleep before a test, you do well. That must be why Mrs. Davis told us to sleep well for our standardized testing. You also can function better in class, not get distracted, and pay attention better. Many positive things come out of sleep. It is also healthy to get enough sleep. A teenager should get at least eight hours of sleep per night. In order to do well in school, I think you should get the maximum number of hours of sleep possible on a school night without unreasonably going to bed at four o'clock pm. ☆

Using Question and Answer to Frame an Argument

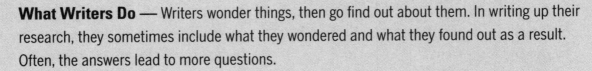

What Writers Do — Writers wonder things, then go find out about them. In writing up their research, they sometimes include what they wondered and what they found out as a result. Often, the answers lead to more questions.

What This Writer Does — In her researched argument about school uniforms, Lorelei clearly demonstrates this process. She states her main point—that school uniforms are good—gives her first reason, backs it up with research, then poses a question that occurs to her. Then she answers that question citing the research she did to find out the answer and writes her new conclusions.

Activity for your class:

1. Read the piece as students follow along on their own copies.

2. Ask students to find Lorelei's original idea, what she wondered, and what she discovered (*the first three sentences in the second paragraph*).

3. Discuss how many students have had the same experience while researching a topic. Share examples. Talk about whether their new questions changed the direction of their final piece.

4. Reflect with the class about how this is often the nature of research and how students might use it to enrich a research project.

Challenge for students:

Think about your school's rules. Write an essay about one rule you think should change. Try the technique that Lorelei used: stating an argument, posing a new question, and supplying the answer.

Using a Question and Answer to Frame an Argument

Opinion	Reasons for opinion	New question	Answer to the question	Restate opinion

There are many reasons to enforce uniforms in schools. One reason is that kids who have less money feel better about who they are. And on top of that not just kids who are less fortunate, but anybody feels better because there are not cool popular brands you have to have, you all wear the same clothes and no one is out of the loop. You're all in the same boat and you all need to get through the rocks and the waves. Teachers, parents and students say that because of the dress code enforcement that the bullying and harassments stop. "80% of parents feel like there is less boy and girl teasing." (Bluesuitmom) Children's grades improve, their work is more readable. Kids care more about the academic reason for school and less about the social aspect of school.

I wonder, if uniforms and dress codes help so much, then why don't more public schools use uniforms? The answer comes from (Frank Nancy). It becomes more work for the school. They have to find a designer, pay them to create a signature look, ship the clothes, distribute them to all the students, create new rules for the uniforms of how they have to be worn, and donate some to the families that can't afford them.

And then after all that is done they will have to deal with at least a few kids to change schools because they don't want to wear uniforms. Although it may seem silly to the most of us, it is not in some other people's minds. It's just something they don't want to do and go through and it doesn't seem like a big deal to them. And now I am not saying that a whole heap of people are going to change schools, but occasionally there would be one or two kids who do. And if it were up to me to lose two students and have better grades from the children and have them much happier or to have two more students and have the kids not as happy, then I choose two less students. Because if we can make school better for the most people then that is the bigger accomplishment, not the amount of students we have in our district. ☆

Editors' Note: Lorelei's bibliographic information has been omitted in the publication of this essay, but the internal citations are included in the text of the essay for demonstration purposes.

Writing a Letter to Raise Awareness About a Social Problem

What Writers Do — Writers are sometimes activists, using the power of language to raise awareness about the world's problems.

What This Writer Does —Madison identifies a problem: stray animals. She then examines the causes of the problem and the effect before offering possible solutions.

Activity for your class:

1. Using highlighters and a copy of the letter, ask individual students or partners to read it and highlight the following:

    - green—problem
    - yellow—causes
    - pink—effects
    - blue—solutions

2. Have students or groups share and discuss their highlighting.

3. As a class, discuss the effectiveness of a letter as a means to address a problem. How does this form compare with an essay that does the same thing?

Challenge for students:

Using the text structure below, write an essay or letter discussing the causes and effects of a problem that has come to your attention. Color-code your final piece the same way you did Madison's letter. Share the results.

Problem Awareness

| Problem | Causes | Effects | Possible solutions |

To: Citizens of Sanantonio@you.net
From: Madison@xyz.com
Re: Don't Delay Stop Strays

Dear Citizens of San Antonio:

I am taking time to write this letter, because this problem is very important to me: strays. I believe that there are way too many strays in this city. For example, the articles you have been seeing in the newspaper about the feral cat population are very concerning.

But do NOT let your pet go in the parks. Have you ever been to Sunken Gardens? The place is overrun with animals. Stray cats, dogs, bunnies, even hamsters! This is one thing people do when they don't want their pets anymore. And most of the animals have diseases. When people go to the parks of San Antonio and see these strays, then that is the memory they will have of our city. Is this the experience San Antonions want people to have?

Another choice is the pet shelter. I would try to avoid this option, because if your pet is there more than three months then they will consider putting it to sleep.

I do not think our pets should suffer the consequence of dying, because of our careless actions. If only we had spayed and neutered. Or if we had taken care of the animal, it would not have to die. Picture your pet as your child. Would you kill your child because you did not want it any more or couldn't take care of it?

With all the strays, it is very expensive for the shelters. The pet shelters are spending a lot of money on each of our lost animals. This money is coming from the city. And then they charge a fee to reunite the family with their pet. As citizens, we pay for this service with our taxes, so now we are paying for our animals twice. Is this the type of city we want to be?

We, as citizens of San Antonio, should be responsible for spaying and neutering our animals. This can be an expensive process but several companies have special dates where they will do it for free. Experts say that spaying and neutering will help reduce strays. ☆

Save our city from strays,

Madison Morris

Using Repetition (Anaphora) for Emphasis and Style

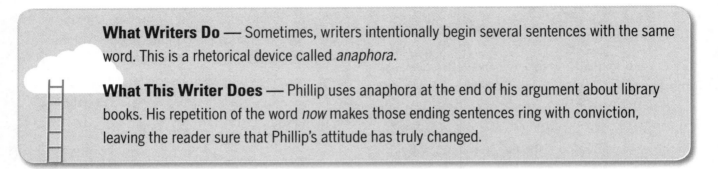

What Writers Do — Sometimes, writers intentionally begin several sentences with the same word. This is a rhetorical device called *anaphora*.

What This Writer Does — Phillip uses anaphora at the end of his argument about library books. His repetition of the word *now* makes those ending sentences ring with conviction, leaving the reader sure that Phillip's attitude has truly changed.

Activity for your class:

1. Read the piece aloud with your class.

2. Ask students what they notice about the last paragraph *(the repetition)*. (Reread it if necessary.)

3. On their copies, have students highlight the word *now* at the beginning of each sentence in the last paragraph.

4. Write *anaphora* (a-NAF-er-uh) on the board and develop a class definition based on Phillip's example. Discuss what effect this has on the piece.

Challenge for students:

Try using anaphora in a piece you are writing. It can be a repeated word or phrase at the beginning of several sentences or clauses. Ask a partner to read your piece aloud and see if you like the effect.

The Story of My Thinking

| What I used to think | But this happened | So now I think |

Why I Like Library Books

I used to think that library books were stupid, with all the due dates and dumb fees. Library books were not good because you get no time to read them. Renewing them is a pain in the behind, and it was not even worth it to check them out. Fuming, I would check out the books knowing that the stupid due dates would get in the way of me reading them! I would be filled with anguish when I had to pay! I would get them just to make my mother happy that I got books! I didn't think I would read them because I would never get to finish them!

But, older and better at reading, I checked out an abundance of books so I wouldn't be bored at my mother's store over summer break. I never actually thought I would finish them. They were really good books and I actually read them. The ones I wouldn't finish, I would renew, and I found out renewing them isn't such a pain in the behind if you do it online. I started to like the library books. They were free, and who doesn't like free stuff? They were really good books, and who doesn't love really good books? And, I didn't have to pay a penny because I just easily renewed them online.

Now, I like library books because they are free, good, and now that I am older, I like to read good books. Now, smiling, I go to the checkout line and I am happy because I get to read good books. Now, libraries are fun. Now, thrilled, I read books and my mother's store isn't as monotonous as it usually is. ☆

Keeping an Argument
From Sliding Into a Personal Narrative

What Writers Do — Writers can use moments from their lives to effectively back up their claims by keeping the anecdotes short. This keeps the writing from turning into a personal narrative and from straying from the primary argument.

What This Writer Does — Tori builds a strong argument about the rudeness of interrupting. She describes several moments from her life to support her points, but by keeping these anecdotes brief, she effectively maintains her focus on the negative impact of interrupting.

Activity for your class:

1. Distribute copies of Tori's piece to the class.

2. Ask students to use highlighters to identify the following:
   - yellow—circle all Tori's personal experiences
   - blue—underline the points she is making in her argument before and after each of her personal anecdotes

3. Discuss with the class.

Challenge for students:

Write an opinion about a pet peeve of yours. Make several points about that pet peeve and include a brief, personal anecdote to support each one. You can use the text structure below or one of your own.

Favorite Activity (Switched to Dislike)

I don't like _____	My first experience with it	How you do it	How it makes you feel	Negative results

Why I Detest Interrupting!!!

I detest interrupting because it's rude and mean. If you want to aggravate someone you interrupt. It may not be beneficial to you though. I have found that teachers detest interrupting more than students usually do. When students interrupt teachers, the teacher will usually give consiquences to the student or the students in the class.

My first experience with this was when I was about 6, and my brother was 3. While I was talking to my dad, all of a sudden a small squeaky voice starts talking. I realized that it was my little brother, Matthew, asking which dinosaur is the biggest. I got really mad and started screaming to my father…"Matthew started talking when I was talking!"

"Matthew, it is impolite to interrupt your sister," my dad replied. "Tell her you're sorry."

Matthew gave me an evil look and said, "Sorry Tori!"

Interrupting can be very easy. You interrupt someone by rudely talking right in the middle of when someone else it talking. For example when your teacher is talking to you or class and you rudely blurt out "But why…?" This is very rude and would even be worse if you whine. That will drive your teacher, and possibly your classmates, insane! Most people find interrupting rude, annoying, and just impolite.

Personally, I absolutely hate when people interrupt me or other people that I'm trying to have a conversation with. When I am asking a teacher such as Ms. Davis about a math problem I hate when someone starts going "Ms. Davis, Ms. Davis! I need help." I don't get so mad that I start screaming. Usually I just stand there, looking at the person that interrupted with an evil glare and thinking "I was here first." Then I wait for her to finish with the other person, if she doesn't ignore them and help me first.

The results of interrupting can be absolutely terrible. Some people will freak out and start screaming at you. Some will start being mean to you if you interrupt them too much. If they really want you to get a taste of your own medicine they will interrupt you until you learn that your interrupting was not appreciated. ☆

Creating a Poster for Persuasion

What Writers Do —Writers sometimes create a poster or a billboard using very few words and one simple image to convey a persuasive message for readers. The illustration captures reader interest in the same way that a great lead does.

What This Writer Does — Will's prohunting poster includes a design that is simple and effective, with a few well-chosen sentences to elegantly convey his point and main reasons.

Activity for your class:

1. Pass out copies of the poster and ask a student with an animated voice to read it aloud.

2. Assign partners or small groups to discuss the following:

   - What is Will's slogan? *(Fire up the grill...cause huntin' ain't catch and release.)*

   - What is his unstated main point? *(Hunting is a good thing.)*

   - What are the author's reasons? *(Hunting helps preserve wildlife and hunting provides delicious food.)*

3. Discuss responses with the class.

Challenge for students:

Think about an issue you are for or against. Create a poster in which you don't state the main point but *show* it in the illustration. Be sure to include a couple of sentences that do show your reasoning. You might want to write a persuasive piece to go with your poster using the text structure below.

What's So Special About This Activity

My opinion about the activity	One thing about the activity	Another thing about the activity	My opinion (once more, with feeling)

FIRE UP THE GRILL...

CAUSE HUNTIN' AIN'T CATCH AND RELEASE...

IT'S PRESERVING WILDLIFE AND
MAKES FOR A DELICIOUS SNACK!!

Using Analogies to Show, Not Tell

What Writers Do — Writers work to create empathy—that is, to help their readers imagine what it is like to be in someone else's shoes. To accomplish this, they use various rhetorical devices. One of these is called an *analogy,* which compares two things.

What This Writer Does — Felicia uses a powerful analogy to help readers feel what is like to be in someone else's shoes. In this way, she does not *tell* them what it's like but *shows* them

Activity for your class:

1. Read the piece aloud as students follow along on their copies.

2. Ask your students to highlight the places in the text where the writer asks the reader to consider another person's point of view (for example, *parents know what teens are going through; parents worry about teens*).

3. Ask: Which example is the most memorable? Which is the one that "got you" the most? *(the baby analogy, probably)*

4. Write the word *analogy* (an-AL-uh-gee) on the board and explain that this is a device for comparing two like things (for example, *the way it feels to try to comfort a crying baby, with the way parents feel helpless with their teenagers sometimes*).

Challenge for students:

Imagine you're Felicia's parent. Write a letter back to her about the points she makes. Try to find places to insert analogies the way Felicia did.

OR

Write a letter to parents of the earth, telling them what you'd like for them to know about teenagers. See what analogies you can work in.

Two Sides of a Coin

Scenario illustrating a problem	Another way to look at the problem	Scenario illustrating the new way to look at the problem	Advice

Dear All Teens on Earth,

"When you get home, I want you to clean up your room, feed the dogs, and put up the clothes on the couch." When I get texts like those from my mom, a chill runs down my spine. Immediately I want to send a text back saying, "YOU HAVE BEEN HOME ALL DAY! WHY CAN'T <u>YOU</u> FEED THE DOGS AND PUT THE CLOTHES UP?!" Anger starts boiling up inside of me because it seems like my parents always know how to really get under my skin. This happens to every teen, right?

I know how parents can be! Trust me, living in the same house as a pastor and his wife isn't always a breeze. We have our moments of what I think is hate. Then, like Texas weather, we become bipolar and act as if we are the happiest family on earth. From my experience, this is true with most teens in the world. But what I always find that is different about me compared to those teens is my personal mindset of my parents.

Now I know what you're thinking, "What do you mean when you say 'mindset'?" Well, I simply mean, what do you think about your parents? My personal thought about my parents is simply that they want to help. They do know what you're going through! You are the first person they have actually had to help get through that rough time called teenage years in one piece. If you think that you are stressed, imagine how tough it must be on them! Everyday when you go to school, they have to worry about the choices you make and your well being. Will you get hurt in P.E. or Athletics? Will you be able to focus on that big exam? These questions haunt their minds until you get back from school.

Have you ever had a really bad day at school? You know, one of those days where when you get home you just want to sit on the couch, ignore all life on earth, and watch T.V.? I know I have! But have you really ever stopped to wonder how that affects your parents? When you have had a bad day, they have to feel the pain you feel PLUS the pain of not knowing how to help. Let me put it this way. Have you ever seen a baby hurt themselves? They cry and scream until the pain subsides. And all the while, you have to hold that baby, helpless and without a clue how to stop the baby's pain. That feeling of helplessness and hopelessness is swimming constantly through your parent's minds whether you choose to believe it or not.

Now, I'm not asking you to be best friends with your parents but what I am going for is simply that you are polite and respect them. Consider their point of view! They want the best for you, and that means they need to punish you and demand things of you to ensure that goal. So, the next time your parents make you resent them, take a deep breath and calm yourself down before you say something you might regret later. Then, (if that didn't help) politely ask if you could walk away and cool off. These methods are a sure-fire way to ensure that you can show and receive respect!

We all want our lives to be easier. It's a proven fact. So how, might you ask, do we accomplish that? The answer is simple. Look at your parents as actual humans with feelings! I know, shocking, right? But the outcome is one that is worth the difficulty. ☆

Thanks for listening!!!

Felicia Valdez

Anticipating and Overcoming Objections

What Writers Do — Writers of persuasive pieces sometimes show their readers how much they understand and respect their readers' opinions, even while working to change their readers' minds.

What This Writer Does —Hagan writes a letter to his father in which he anticipates the questions his father might ask if they were having a discussion. He then answers those questions. This is also called overcoming objections.

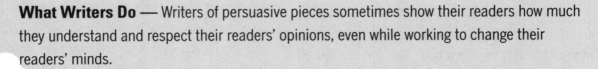

Activity for your class:

1. Using a copy of the letter, ask students to underline the sentences in which Hagan anticipates his father's thinking.

2. Then have them circle Hagan's responses to his father's objections.

3. Discuss with the class.

Challenge for students:

Imagine you are Hagan's father. Write a matching "Dear Son" letter. You can decide what his answer will be, but be sure to use the same tactic Hagan did: anticipating questions and answering them to overcome objections.

OR

Write a letter asking someone to change his or her mind. Show that you understand your reader's position and work to overcome anticipated objections. The text structure below might be used as a starting point.

Making a Request

My request	One way this will help	Another way this will help	Why now is the right time	The question for you to answer

Part III. Opinion/Argument

Dear Dad,

I have asked for more money than usual lately and there is a reason; I am really asking for a bigger allowance. I know you will probably want to hear why I need more money, since there isn't a lot to go around. So I came up with some reasons you might like. If you did give me a raise on my allowance I would put one fourth of it in my bank account (for emergencies or a new car in my future), after all, I do need to think ahead, right? The rest of the money would be my spending money for—what else—spending! Don't worry, I'm responsible, I will keep track of the spending money and never lose it. If I can keep track of my phone, my schoolwork and my brother at the same time, I think I can keep track of my wallet in my back pocket.

My next reason isn't selfish. If you did give me more money on my allowance I will have enough money to make donations and help people in need. I'll try my best to do the chores you give me and I'll do double the work whenever you tell me. Oh and remember what I said about donations to people? I would be happy to loan you money whenever you need it. I will try even harder at school work, I'll do the extra-credit assignments and focus even more in school. The work may be hard, but I can get through it.

I know you would want to know what I would be spending all my money on and I have an answer. There are a lot of things I would like to have but I want to spend my money wisely, so I want to save up for a new television for my room. I barely spend any time up there so I decided why not just get more excitement into my boring room. I know you think I'll blow it all off on candy like that one time when I was seven, but I'm thirteen. I can be patient. Remember when I was saving up for that video game? Riley was saving up for another game so we were having a little compatition to see who would break and blow their money off first. Guess who

won? Me! I saved up for the game but had to loan it to Riley so he would have the game he wanted (out of the goodness of my heart, I might add). After all that I think I have shown you I have patience to save up and the responsibility to make decisions.

I have told you how I am responsible enough to make decisions and to keep track of the money. I think I should tell you that I'm trusted enough to be wise with it. Though I might be tempted to spend the money on other things, I'll be able to manage. I remember when I was about 4, I had been saving up for a bike but then I saw these little footballs with candy in them. I spent all my money on the candy but I did learn something: you have to be patient with saving, you need to learn to wait.

We all get tempted but some of us are able to just say no to ourselves, even if it's hard to. I don't want to force you to give me more money. It's your choice, I will leave it to you. Before you decide, however, know this, I will try my hardest in school and still do my work even if you say no.

To you I might seem selfish...but considering what I've told you, do you think I'm responsible? ☆

Hagan Cousin

Anticipating a Reader's Objections

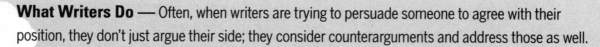

What Writers Do — Often, when writers are trying to persuade someone to agree with their position, they don't just argue their side; they consider counterarguments and address those as well.

What This Writer Does — While setting up his argument, Stetson uses his knowledge about his mother to anticipate her objections and then smoothly address them.

Activity for your class:

1. Ask students to read the piece with a partner.

2. Have them highlight one or two phrases that show what Stetson's mother might be thinking, such as *"...you find it pointless..." "You think me playing guitar is just a phase..."*

3. Next, ask them to draw a stick figure of Stetson's mom in the margin. Add word bubbles with comments his mom might be making, for example, *"You've only had your guitar for five months!"*

4. Invite students to draw this conversation as a comic strip between Stetson and his mom.

Challenge for students:

Look at one of your own pieces of persuasive writing, or write a new one using the "sales pitch" text structure. Try anticipating some reactions your audience might have if they were able to talk back to you. Overcome their objections. Then, try drawing your argument as a comic strip.

Making a Sales Pitch

One reason you may object to my plan	My plan	What I will do to prove you wrong	How we will celebrate if I am right

Dear Mum,

I know I just got a new guitar five months ago and you find it pointless to buy me another one since I've been playing for a short amount of time. You think me playing guitar is just a phase and that I'll grow out of it soon when the reality is I love it even more as time goes on. I have come a long way from my pee-wee fender and am still learning. However I feel like I am ready to "upgrade" so to speak. I have been looking online and in pawn stores. I found one online at sweetwater.com that I feel would be good for me at my level. It's a high-valued brand but is nice and cheap. It's a Black Epiphone special two les paul edition. It comes with a gig case and amp. All together it's worth $500 dollars but is being sold for $200 dollars. It comes with two humbucking pick-ups which help the tone quality.

I know my guitar "career" is short and you're unsure if I'll stick with it, but it would help me learn new techniques. I love guitar and lose myself in the music I make. I'll happily show you how far I've come. I know I can't shred yet but I'm on my way. Plus wouldn't it be awesome for your son to be a world famous rocker!? I'm not saying we buy me a PRS that run for about $5,000 dollars, but one that would help me improve.

I think we should set up a day where the whole family comes to see me play. I'd love it and it would get me comfortable with playing for crowds. How cool would it be to sit in the "front row" at my first concert? For free! It'd be an awesome oppurtunity for everyone. Like I said I don't want to go all out....I'm just suggesting we give room to grow and improve as a musician and human being. ☆

Sincerely

Your son, The Rocker

Using Hyperbole for Effect

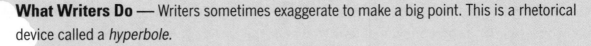

What Writers Do — Writers sometimes exaggerate to make a big point. This is a rhetorical device called a *hyperbole.*

What This Writer Does —In this essay about his favorite sports hero, Jeret uses well-placed hyperbole to emphasize why Nolan Ryan is his role model.

Activity for your class:

1. Read the piece together with the class.

2. Ask students to circle the first two sentences on their copies.

3. Ask: "Do you think Jeret meant for those sentences to be taken literally or figuratively?"

4. Write *hyperbole* (hy-PER-buh-lee) on the board and explain that this is a type of figurative language that exaggerates something with an extreme example.

5. Have students work to rephrase the sentence using the literal speed of the ball. Discuss the difference in effect—and the effectiveness of hyperbole used well.

Challenge for students:

Using the text structure below, or another one of your choice, write about a person you admire. Experiment with hyperbole in your piece. Share.

Why I Admire Someone

Whom I admire	Internal characteristics of that person	External skills he or she has	The effect this person has on me

Part III. Opinion/Argument

One would think that being superhuman is impossible, but that is exactly what Nolan Ryan once was. He could throw a baseball at the speed of light. That is why he is a role model to me.

Nolan Ryan, unlike many other professional baseball players, does not boast and try to show off. He is honest and tries his hardest every game. Even though he was one of the greatest, he knew he still had more to learn. When he steps up to the pitcher's mound, he goes up with confidence and composure. Even though he strikes out most of them, he does not laugh in their faces.

Nolan Ryan has always been one of my favorite role models; my dad is a big fan of him too. I learned everything I know from watching videos and clips of him pitching. I have watched his strategy and technique on how to think like the batter, and how to keep the batters off-guard. When he pitches, he uses his whole body, his legs, arms, and core to throw lightning bolts. This extraordinary person has made a difference in my life because of his actions and attitude toward being successful in life. He has made me a better person and better at baseball. ☆

Discovering a Problem, Proposing a Solution

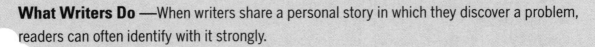

What Writers Do —When writers share a personal story in which they discover a problem, readers can often identify with it strongly.

What This Writer Does —Jordan shares how he noticed the litter problem and how he took action on his own. Since his efforts didn't solve the problem, he suggests some new ideas for his readers to consider.

Activity for your class:

1. Give students copies of Jordan's letter and read it together. As a class, discuss who Mr. Davis might be *(the mayor, his principal)*.

2. Have students highlight each sentence in which Jordan describes:
   - yellow—all about Jordan and his experience
   - green—all about the world beyond Jordan's family
   - blue—Jordan's new ideas for solving the problem

Challenge for students:

Think of a time when you tried to change something and realized the problem was too big. Write that story. Be sure to include new solutions that occurred to you because of your experiences.

Problem/Solution

How I noticed the problem	Effort that did not work	How big the problem is	A possible solution

Dear Mr. Davis,

One day my dad and I were sitting at our house with nothing to do when he asked me if I wanted to ride bikes to the park. I said, "Sure." Then we left. While riding I noticed all the trash on the side of the road. I asked him, "Why would people want to make their own city look so bad?" He said, "Why don't you do something about it instead of riding bikes?" I said, "Okay," and we went back home to put our bikes away and get some trash bags and gloves. We went back to the park an hour later and there seemed to be even more trash than before. We started on Poetry Road at one o'clock in the afternoon and did not stop until eight o'clock in the evening, and the bad thing was we didn't even finish!

The next day we finished, and as we were walking off these high school kids that were driving by threw some bottles on the ground. I think they saw that my dad and I had the bags full of trash because they were pointing at us and laughing. I think that something should be done about this thing called littering, don't you?

I mean it is not just people that are getting hurt but animals as well. The animals might mistake a wrapper as food and try to eat it. Many things could happen to the animals if they try to eat the trash, too. The first thing is that they could choke on it. If they are lucky enough to swallow it then they will probably not be able to digest it. So either way they would die just because somebody decided that they wanted to throw some trash on the ground.

Here is an idea that might work. Maybe if you see somebody littering then you should have to report them, and if you don't then you should be punished just as bad as the person that committed the crime. If we can get every citizen to do this, then we could make the streets of Terrell clean. This would not just make travelers think that our city is clean, but it will even give the citizens something to be proud of. Like if somebody's family came to town they wouldn't want their family to think that they live in a bad or dirty city, because I know when my family comes to Terrell, I want them to think this is the best city in the world. ☆

Sincerely,

Jordan Powell

Weaving Information
Into a Persuasive Argument

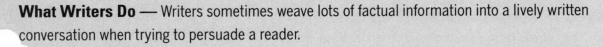

What Writers Do — Writers sometimes weave lots of factual information into a lively written conversation when trying to persuade a reader.

What This Writer Does — Katie embeds the detailed rules about her school's uniforms into her letter to her principal. This clarifies the situation for readers who might not be familiar with the rules without including a boring list.

Activity for your class:

1. Give students copies of Katie's letter.

2. Have them make a list of the dress code regulations at Katie's school.

3. Compare and discuss. Decide which would be more persuasive: attaching the list of rules to the letter or embedding the information the way Katie did.

Challenge for students:

Write a letter about a school policy or rule you'd like to see changed. Make sure to embed the facts and details about that rule into your persuasive letter the way Katie did. The text structure below might help you get started.

Opinion Piece

Opinion because of A, B, C	How I know A	How I know B	How I know C	Restate opinion

Dear Mr. Frank Alexander,

I remember last week when my friend came over and was going through my closet. She thinks I have a fashion sense...I don't know where she gets that from. Then all of a sudden the smile on her face turned into disgust. She pulled out a pair of pants and a shirt from my lower hook. She stared at them and asked what this was supposed to be. I said it was my school uniform.

Red, white, or navy blue shirts. Khaki pants, blue pants, and/or shorts. When put together it looks very neat and spiffy, but it really isn't the type of clothes that teenagers would wear. When you think about it, the dress code isn't all that bad. But the rules about it are horrible!

Wearing these uniforms takes away all of the individuality of each and every student attending the school. Since we are forced to wear the pants and shirt, oh and lets not forget about the brown or black belt, we should be allowed to show our personality. Shouldn't we? Being stuck in this dress code makes it kinda hard...

We aren't allowed to have little designs on our shirts, even if it's smaller than a dime and in the corner! Then, our shorts are very strict, SHORTS! They have to be above the knee, or else they are considered as capris (which aren't allowed), then if they are shorter than your finger tips then they are too short. As for pants, they must cover our ankles, or they are capris, which you already read, AREN'T allowed.

Even our jackets have to be red, white, or navy blue. We can't have cute jackets with rhinestones or designs. I think that the dress code rules are a little too strict. Like I mentioned before, there is no way for the students to show their personality and creativeness.

So, Mr. Alexander, the next time that the school board comes by and asks about the uniform, or says that they are going to add more rules...think about all of your students that attend Terrell Independent School Districts. What would they say if they were there, with you? ☆

Signed,

Katie Weishaar
Herman Furlough Middle School
7th Grade

Writing a Descriptive Lead

What Writers Do — Writers may begin with a poetic image (sometimes employing metaphors and similes), painting a picture that helps us see the subject before they tell us their main point.

What This Writer Does —Kazmine, Kagen, and Melody each write about their role model, using extraordinary, descriptive leads. Readers are hooked before they get to the thesis statement.

Activity for your class:

1. Ask three different student volunteers to read the three leads out loud.

2. Discuss the following questions, making a list of answers on the board:
   - What did all three writers do first? *(Describe the person's appearance.)*
   - What did all three writers do next? *(Describe the person's character traits.)*
   - Where did they write their thesis statements? *(One at the beginning, one at the end, one not at all [it is implied].)*

3. Discuss the elements of these descriptive leads as a class: What is behind their effectiveness? Where could you use similarly descriptive leads?

4. Have students try writing a similar lead about someone they admire. Share.

Challenge for students:

Try writing an essay about someone you admire, and include a paragraph modeled on the text structure below. See where the paragraph works best in your piece.

Writing a Descriptive Lead

A person I'm close to	Three physical descriptions	Two inner character traits

---

Kazmine Godwin, Kagen Burkett, and Melody Johns – Grade 7

My grandpa with his white beard and thin figure is my role model. He is aged, wise, and has a memory as sharp as a tack. My grandpa is the laugh in my happiness.

—*Kazmine*

Her skin is dark from a life of hard work in the heat of the sun. She is an elderly lady with hands dried and cracked from her work. She is a good Christian lady and has faith in God's greater plan. By our church family she is known as Sister Nell, but to me, she is known as Maw Maw.

—*Kagen*

My grandma has hair the color of a gray crayon, and she is a tall glass of water. She makes my smile a mile long every time she speaks, and most of all, her heart couldn't get any bigger. My grandma is my role model. ☆

—*Melody*

Using Third-Person Examples in an Argument

What Writers Do — Writers cite examples from the real world and not just their own personal experiences to make a point.

What This Writer Does — Nick creates an argument that advocates for the use of cell phones in school. He uses third-person examples to illustrate his points, the way writers of articles do.

Activity for your class:

1. Read the piece aloud to the class after passing out copies.

2. Give the following directions, allowing time for partners or groups to discuss as they work:

   - Using highlighters, color the following sentences:
     - yellow—Nick's main point, or his position (*smart phones are an extremely useful wireless device in school*)
     - green—Nick's three reasons (*useful websites, educational games, parent communication*)
   - Next, circle his example for each reason.
   - After that, underline the subject of each example (*Reid, José, I*).

3. Share responses. Discuss together how the first two examples use the third person to refer to other people (*Reid and José*).

4. Talk about how this argument would have been different if the author had used *I* for all three reasons.

Challenge for students:

Write an argument advocating for something important to you. Build in third-person examples. You can refer to the text structure below if you need help with organization.

Advocating for Something

Opinion because of A, B, C	How I know A	How I know B	How I know C	Restate opinion

Smart phones are an extremely useful wireless device in school that are as speedy as a cheetah.

These phones have useful websites for school. Instead of going home and using the computer to do his homework, Reid pulls out his I-phone during advisory and watches the math video for tonight.

Another reason is some games are educational. In science class José took out his phone yesterday when his teacher was done teaching, and played his favorite game Levers and Pulleys.

Finally you need a phone to communicate to your parents about after school activities. One day I didn't know when tutoring ended, so I had to wait two hours until I got home, but if I had a smart phone my mom could have come and picked me up.

Yes, we use phones to communicate outside of school, but smart phones are an extremely useful wireless device in school. ☆

97

Using Opposites (Antithesis) to Make an Impact

What Writers Do — Writers use rhetorical devices because they can have a powerful effect on a reader. One of these is *antithesis* (an-TITH-uh-sis), a move in which writers use opposites within a sentence to make an impact

What This Writer Does —Toni skillfully uses antithesis throughout her piece, adding depth and voice to her imaginative letter informing "Teens of the World" about the dangers of alcohol.

Activity for your class:

1. Ask a volunteer to read the piece aloud to the class while they follow along.

2. Assign different paragraphs to small groups or partners. Tell students to look for sentences that start with one thought and then switch to its opposite in some way. Use highlighters to show this:

   - yellow—the first thought in the sentence
   - green—the opposite thought that follows (for example, *"I wish I were able to say that my mother was my role model, but then I'd be lying; I love her, I really do, it's just I'm saddened by her horrid actions; I don't know if…but all I know is…; good for some, bad for others"*)

3. Share examples aloud and listen for the opposites. Discuss the impact they make on the essay.

Challenge for students:

Revisit something that you have written. See if you can work on a few sentences, revising them to use *antithesis* in your constructions. Decide whether you consider the piece to be improved by the use of this device.

Making a Promise to Change Something

Zoom in on one person's story	Problems this person has	How the problem affects everyone	What I promise to do to change it

Dear Teens of the World,

I write to you today about a woman named Angel Zimmerman. You may be wondering who this unfamiliar stranger is...well I'll tell you. Angel is my biological mother and one of the worlds many alcoholics. I wish I were able to say that my mother was my role model, but then I'd be lying.

Today I watch her grow older from a distance all because of one life threat...alcohol. I love her, I really do, it's just I'm saddened by her horrid actions. My friends say not to worry about it, and that's she is just having fun, but they have NO idea.

Also, because of alcohol my mother became pregnant at the age of 16. I'm glad she did, because if she wouldn't have been impregnated I would not have my wonderful sister, Destinni. I don't know if that's what my mom, Angel, wanted or not, but all I know is how many opportunities were ruined for her. She couldn't be a cheerleader or athlete even though she wasn't very interested in sports, but she could have the amazing opportunity of having a family.

I believe that drinking alcohol can go either way. Good for some, bad for most. I say good for some, meaning the ones who watch the consumers of the poisnous, adicting beverage can see what not to do, and they can learn from other's mistakes, instead of making the life changing mistake themselves. You could have such a better life and more great opportunities without the dangerous beverage, in my opinion.

From my experience of watching my mother, I have gained independence for myself. No longer do or will I be a follower of the so called "cool kids." I will lead my school to right desicions and hopefully one day lead the entire nation to be an alcohol free republic. I plan to touch others with my words and actions by doing what I believe instead of just being a by stander who watches things go wrong and wish that I could fix them. Instead I, Toni Zimmerman will fix problems until one day those problems may not exist. ☆

You'll remember me,

Toni Zimmerman

Revising an Argument for Length

What Writers Do — Professional writers may finish a piece and then discover that a publisher needs it to be shorter to fit into their publication. This happens often in printed materials like newspapers, magazines, or books. Even student writers are sometimes given length limitations.

What This Writer Does —Tyler's piece is a wonderful but lengthy argument urging people to think differently and take better care of our planet. He begins with disturbing information about the great Pacific trash heap and ends with effective "garden of Eden" images. In between, he provides multiple descriptions of the problem, as well as solutions.

Activity for your class:

1. Give this task to groups of students after giving them copies:

    "Imagine you are newspaper editors, and you would like to publish this on the editorial page. The problem is that it needs to be about one page long in order to fit into the newspaper column's space. This means trimming it by half. Your job is to shorten this piece. Keep the beginning and ending, and focus on trimming the middle. You may delete words, phrases, or paragraphs. You may also combine sentences."

2. Compare the results. Ask students to explain their editing choices.

Challenge for students:

Try this editing exercise on one of your own longer pieces, or write a new one about an environmental problem using the text structure below. See if editing it for length improves it.

Alerting Reader to a Problem

Visual image of problem	What will happen in the future	One plan	Attitude change required	Imagine if...

Dear People of the Earth,

Have you ever heard of the Great Pacific trash heap? It's this huge mass of trash that is trapped by the sea's currents. The trash can't decompose. Therefore it has gotten big enough to cover the state of Texas twice! This has become a huge problem because animals that live there constantly get caught in the garbage and either die due to starvation, or have to evacuate the area leaving the ecosystem unbalanced, causing certain species to overpopulate.

More and more of this type of thing will occur in the future if we don't do something soon. Wildlife will wither, the ocean will become nothing more than a giant sludge pool and the forests will become huge landfills. Millions of animals have already become subject to man's incapability to care. Why make it worse?

What I'm suggesting might sound crazy to some people, but the fact is that we just aren't trying hard enough to take care of our Earth. Something us students can do is maybe set a day in the month to gather and pick up trash along the highway. I believe this would make a huge difference.

Little things like aluminum cans or plastic bags add up and we can't keep adding to the equation. Hundreds of species are endangered because of our species. We think we are so much better than every other animal, but do they pollute and destroy our environment?

It takes a special kind of person to see a bottle on the side of the road and pull over to pick it up. Another thing it takes a special person to do is, see a turtle crawling across the road, pick it up and move it over to the other side. Little things like that make all the difference.

From the beginning all we've ever done is care about ourselves and never taken in consideration the effects of our actions. It's about time we did something about attitude. Try to use greener options like using real plates instead of plastic ones. If it's possible take quick showers instead of baths (it doesn't use as much water). If you want to take it to the next step, another thing that you can do is look around and see what you can do in your community.

So next time you're driving down the road or playing at the beach, think about the cause and effect of, for example, throwing a candy wrapper out the window or onto the sand. Think about the innocent lives you might cause to suffer for it. How would you like it if you swallowed a bottle cap because you thought it was your dinner? How would you like it if you were covered head to toe in crude oil?

If we could help clean and maintain our environment, we could save ourselves and billions of other living organisms from a hell on Earth. Just imagine crystal clear waters teaming with life. Forests overflowing with vegetation and inspiration. Earth would be an Oasis that we could enjoy for generations to come. A garden of Eden we could all share. ☆

Sincerely,

Tyler Moore

Using the Literary Present Tense to Present an Argument

What Writers Do — Writers are often asked to analyze the merits of literary works. When discussing particular events from a work, writers may use the present tense to give their arguments a sense of immediacy.

What This Writer Does — Brittany makes the argument that the element of surprise is the successful ingredient in the novel *The Hunger Games.* In her analysis, she skillfully employs the literary present tense to strengthen her argument.

Activity for your class:

1. Read the piece together after students receive a copy.

2. Ask the class to look at the second paragraph and underline the verbs.

3. Then assign paragraphs to different sections of the class to rewrite in the past tense.

4. Read revisions aloud. Discuss how these slight differences in the sentences change the tone of the argument. Which way seems stronger?

Challenge for students:

Think about a book you have read recently and choose a moment that you considered one of the best moments in the book. Tell about that moment using the literary present. Develop it into a complete essay if you wish using the text structure below.

Making a Claim With Four Examples

Claim	Example 1	Example 2	Example 3	Example 4	Conclusion

Suzanne Collins' Unexpected Tricks to Perfecting *Mockingjay*

Every once in a blue moon I sit myself down to read a good book. It might just be me or is it that it's extremely hard to find a book that you fall in love with or you're just addicted to? To most people it's so easy to pick a book but to me it's like finding a needle in a hay stack. Fortunately I have finally found one of the best novels in the history of my fourteen years. Every single author always incorporates tricks into their novels to keep all readers glued to their pieces. Unlike most, the amazingly talented author Suzanne Collins uses one trick that makes her pieces so unique...the element of surprise. Throughout *Mockingjay* not once have I ever expected so many surprises to come my way. Every single time I'm about to finish a chapter the author takes an unexpected twist.

Throughout the series of the *Hunger Games*, Katniss Everdeen and Peeta Mellark are passionately in love with each other and are destined to be with each other forever. No matter how bad the situation is they will do everything to keep each other alive and to be safely in each other's arms. In her third book *Mockingjay*, Peeta is suddenly captured by the capitol after the revolution breaks out throughout all twelve districts when the tributes are fighting to the death during the 25th annual Quarter Quell.

As all the surviving tributes are moved into the lost district of thirteen Katniss awakes from her hospital bed to find out what is happening and what has happened to her beloved Peeta. When Peeta is rescued from the city of Panem he is returned to district thirteen. While in rehabilitation Katniss visits Peeta and before she even gets to say hello she is struggling to breathe with Peeta's hand around her neck. Katniss finds out that Peeta has been brainwashed by the capitol with trackerjacker venom and he is convinced that she's out to kill him. While reading the last two pages of this chapter my heart sank. This situation takes a giant turn in the entire story. How will they take down the capitol? How will they get revenge on President Snow? How will they ever be together?

While Katniss is trying to forget about Peeta she visits district two to help out any survivors from the massive attacks by the capitol. Katniss and her team make a plan to blow up one of the important mountains where all the carriers work "The Nut." Suddenly Katniss is surrounded by armed carriers who have made their way out of the explosion. While she is giving her speech about how she is not the enemy but the capitol is the enemy she is shot. This small one line sentence produced hundreds of questions and once again Suzanne Collins uses the element of surprise and fear to change the entire plot.

By orders Katniss and her team are stationed in the Capitol. Day and night she learns new military tactics and is also getting better from her injury. Haymitch gives commands to make a Mockingjay video to get all the districts aware of the rebellion that is occurring. While filming the video with fake bombs, loud machine guns, and troop 451 not taking the video seriously Boggs their commander turns to them to pull it together and suddenly his legs are blown off by a landmine. From laughter to shrieks and screams the entire plot once again is changed.

Suzanne Collins is a phenomenal author because she has kept thousands of fans reading and reading. Her tricks that she uses are simple: the element of surprise, characters that you instantly fall in love with, fear, gets your adrenaline going, and she is always turning tables. Throughout this book I have never been bored because the entire time I am always being surprised and wanting to read more. ☆

Making Inferences From Pictures

> **What Writers Do** — Writers sometimes explore an image, making discoveries and drawing insights that lead their readers to see things in a new light.
>
> **What This Writer Does** — Barrett begins with a truism (life lesson) about the importance of family and then uses a newspaper photograph to illustrate his discovery about his grandmother and his family heritage.

Activity for your class:

1. Distribute copies of Barrett's piece to the class and read it together.

2. Discuss Barrett's discovery *(his grandmother's story and photo with President Eisenhower)* and insight *(his first and last sentences)*.

3. Ask students to draw a 5-minute sketch of the photo that Barrett described, being sure to include the headline over the photo.

4. Discuss Barrett's truism "Our families help make us who we are" with the class. Ask: "Do you agree or disagree? Why or why not?"

Challenge for students:

Bring in a picture or draw a sketch of an important moment in your life (or in a story). Use the Picture Proof text structure below to write about it. Begin or end with Barrett's truism or one of your own.

Picture Proof

Description of a picture of an important moment	This picture makes me realize that...	Truism

Believe in Yourself

When you hear about how your grandparents have done something amazing or how your parents have done something that you thought was impossible, you begin to believe that you can do something like that, you believe that you can do something even better.

My grandmother told me a story about how she was an Airline Stewardess. She told me once that she was on the same plane as President Eisenhower. When the paper came out with a picture of them standing together, the headline read "Faye Hardy and friend!" and she was standing with President Eisenhower.

Our families can make us think we can do or be anything. This makes me wonder if people with boring parents may have a boring life themselves.

Our families help make us who we are. ☆

Supporting an Argument
With Expert Knowledge

What Writers Do — Writers choose topics that they know very well, using specific details to show their expert knowledge.

What This Writer Does — Ben presents five different reasons to convince the reader that hog hunting is important. With each one, he paints a different picture that the reader can visualize. His expert knowledge is clear and strengthens his argument.

Activity for your class:

1. Read and discuss Ben's essay after giving each student a copy.

2. Invite students to draw a stick-figure cartoon panel showing one of Ben's five reasons and examples.

3. Post the cartoons around the classroom or in a hall. Hold a gallery walk to identify each reason. Discuss how the details support Ben's argument.

Challenge for students:

Think of something that you have spent a lot of time doing. List the reasons people should do it, giving clear examples from your personal knowledge and experience. Write an essay or draw a cartoon strip based on your reasons.

Expert Opinion

Topic and position	Reasons with clear examples	Restate your position once more with feeling

Top 5 Reasons for Hunting Hogs

The reason hunting hogs is so important is because whether you're a rancher or a deer hunter, hogs just mess things up. They will always break everything you have and scare the deer.

Any deer hunter knows that the worst thing while you're deer hunting is to see your deer run off only to see a pack of hogs walk out snorting and squealing as they snobbily eat all the corn. Therefore this brings me to give you the top 5 reasons why we hunt hogs to get rid of them.

The first reason is by tearing up the deer feeder. The hogs will always get wild while they are eating corn and end up breaking either a side or some part of a feeder that I will have to fix.

The second reason is because the hogs will scare away the deer at a feeder. The deer don't like being around them so right when they see one they run. I had one time where this huge buck just walked out and I was about to take him when a big ole pack of hogs came out to the feeder.

The third reason is because they will break fences. Hogs like to travel, so when they come upon a fence they have to get through it. They all will bust it open and leave a big hole in the fence.

The fourth reason is for when it has just rained a lot. What the hogs love the most is making mud holes out in a field. They will roll around and make a deep hole to mess around in. Once the mud dries there are holes everywhere that mess up all the crops.

And the last reason is that when you have a water tank you don't want hogs getting into it and messing it up to where the water might go out of the tank and drain off to the side. So if you're both a rancher and a hunter, you have plenty of reasons to hunt down those hogs. ☆

Appendix A: 25 Ways to Use Great Student Essays

So you've collected a great group of papers from *your* students.

In the old days, we used to just read them and say "Ahh." Those days are gone. Now they're incredible teaching tools, far better than anything we could buy.

So what can you do with them with your class?

1. Read one aloud and see what kids notice.

2. Chunk one into parts, summarize the parts, and draw boxes to show the text structure of that piece.

3. Find one with great linking (structure) and convert it to a template for imitation. For more information, see the "Timothy Toad" lesson (Lesson 37).

4. Devolve one. For more information, see "Devolving an Essay" at www.trailofbreadcrumbs.net.

5. Read openings and listen to the variety.

6. List genres of samples you find.

7. Make a chart of strong verbs.

8. Make posters of your school's best papers and line up that great work in a "hall of fame" display. (You'll need permission from the authors and their parents to post the students' names.)

9. Get a "How I did it" commentary from writers and post annotations with the essay.

10. Look at interesting punctuation across several papers.

11. Find essays with very different voices, and read several aloud. Ask students to describe the differences in voices.

12. Type up one without any punctuation, and try to read it aloud. Compare it to its original.

13. Look at dialogue across several papers.

14. Do a highlighter hunt for brushstrokes (for more information on brushstrokes, see Harry Noden's *Image Grammar.*)

15. Have students draw what they hear.

16. Underline every other sentence, and read with two voices. Listen for variety in sentence lengths.

17. Do a vocal color-coding: Listen to the first four words in every sentence, in alternating voices.

18. Make a labyrinth on the floor, with corners holding examples of whatever you find in the gorgeous essays, like extraordinary vocabulary, striking verbs, or rhetorical devices. Then use it as a "walk" for students writing their own essays.

19. Devolve one sentence from specific to general.

20. Read one aloud, and write letters to the author.

21. Do a highlighter hunt for truisms or life lessons.

22. Do a highlighter hunt for ba-da-bing sentences (see Gretchen's book *Reviving the Essay: How to Teach Structure Without Formula* for more on ba-da-bing sentences).

23. Use opening lines as starters for student essays.

24. Draw or map out the text structure.

25. Search for words from the prompt to see where or if they appear in the piece.

Appendix B: Text Structures

Advocating for Something

Opinion because of A, B, C	How I know A	How I know B	How I know C	Restate opinion

Alerting Reader to a Problem

Visual image of problem	What will happen in the future	One plan	Attitude change required	Imagine if...

All About an Event

How the event started	What we eat and why	One object we use	Something we read or sing	Why I like it so much

Anadiplosis

Truism chain	My dream (why I had it)	How I started to achieve the dream	How I finally reached the dream	Truism chain

Book Review

Information about publication	Favorite lines, with commentary	Information about characters, setting, plot	Recommendation

Change Proclamation in Epistolary Form

Letter proclaiming a change	Why the change is needed	How the change will help	Letter of response from someone affected by the change

Character Clashes

Description of problem between characters	Example 1	Example 2	Example 3	What these create for the reader

Clues and Confirmation

| What I was afraid was happening | Some clues that told me this | Some more clues that told me | How I finally knew the truth |

Comparing Notes

| Some people think... | And other people think... | But I think... | What that tells me |

A Completely Made-Up Story

| Characters doing something | Problem arises | How they try to solve it | How they do solve it |

A Completely Made-Up Story With Cliffhanger for Sequel

| Characters doing something | Problem arises | How they try to solve it | How they solve it | A new problem |

Conversation Between Characters

Question from one character	Answer from another character	Author's blurb: why you chose those characters

Cubing an Object for an "All About" Essay

Describe it	How it is used	What it is like/unlike	How it can change	What it can cause

Defining the Meaning of a Concept

General meaning of the word	A moment from my life illustrating the word	What that moment taught me about the word	My own deeper meaning of the word

Describing a Character

This character is (description)	One way we know (with quotes and explanations)	Another way we know (with quotes and explanations)	These all add up to show us this

Development of a Friendship

| My wrong first impression | Moment of bonding | One moment you taught me an important lesson | Another moment you taught me an important lesson | Ways you've become my most important friend |

Directly Addressing a Dreaded Concept

| How most people see you | How I see the opposite | How people resist you | How much we actually need you | My words of encouragement to you |

Doing Something Well 101

| Truism | Step 1 | Step 2 | Step 3 | Step 4 | Results |

Downfall

| How bad things are now | Flashback to happier days | Details about how bad things are now | My feelings now |

    Fun-Size Academic Writing for Serious Learning

Drumming Up Support

Problem		Why we should face it		What we must do

Expert Opinion

Topic and position		Reasons with clear examples		Restate your position once more with feeling

Favorite Activity (Switched to Dislike)

I don't like _____	My first experience with it	How you do it	How it makes you feel	Negative results

Four Points and Their Effect

One thing that has this effect	Another thing that has this effect	Another thing that has this effect	One more thing that has this effect	How they all add up to create the same effect

Full Analysis Using "Questioning the Author"

Intro	+ (	Questioning the Author	× 3) +	Conclusion

Questioning the Author:
- I'd ask ____
- Because I read "____"
- I thought ____

History of Something (Event)

Why this happened	When it happened	What people thought then	What I think now

The Importance of Something

Its physical properties	What it means to me	What I did	What I discovered

Knocking Down the Opposition

Opinion/ argument	1st objection that people have (and why it's wrong)	2nd objection that people have (and why it's wrong)	3rd objection that people have (and why it's wrong)	Restatement and call to action

Fun-Size Academic Writing for Serious Learning

Letter Exchange Between Two Characters

Letter from 1st character	Letter back from 2nd character	Letter back from 1st character	Repeat as much as you want

Making a Claim About a Historical Event

Event	Why this happened	When it happened	What people thought then	What I think now

Making a Claim With Four Examples

Claim	Example 1	Example 2	Example 3	Example 4	Conclusion

Making a Promise to Change Something

Zoom in on one person's story	Problems this person has	How the problem affects everyone	What I promise to do to change it

Making a Request

| My request | One way this will help | Another way this will help | Why now is the right time | The question for you to answer |

Making a Sales Pitch

| One reason you may object to my plan | My plan | What I will do to prove you wrong | How we will celebrate if I am right |

Memory Reflection

| Where you were | What happened first | What happened next | What happened last | What you thought |

Memory Reflection (Mixed Feelings)

| Where you were | What happened first and how you felt | What happened next and how you felt differently | What happened last and how you felt | What you thought |

Memory Reflection With Onomatopoeia

	(Bang)	(Pow)	(Zoom)	
Where you were	What happened first	What happened next	What happened last	What you thought

Movie Self-Discussion

A movie I watched	A history connection	What the movie was really about	What the title might mean	What I wonder

Multimedia Literary Analysis of a Theme

A theme from the literature	A poem, showing the theme (with quotes)	A drawing or painting, illustrating your interpretation of that theme in the literature	My explanation: how I constructed the poem or painting just as I did; how I made choices and what I think they show

Now Introducing Something

One person's moment using it	What problem it solves	How it works	But one problem it creates	Reason it is a good idea anyway	Published data about it

One Thing the Character Would Like to Know About

| She or he sometimes wonders about... | She or he knows that _____ (and how) | She or he also knows _____ (and how) | She or he can't figure out how... | So she or he plans to... |

Opinion Piece

| Opinion because of A, B, C | How I know A | How I know B | How I know C | Restate opinion |

Opinion Piece About a Historical Figure

| Why I chose the person | One quality he or she had | One moment I saw that quality | How that affected the people | My opinion about the person |

Personifying an Abstract

| _____ is what kind of person | What she or he does around others | What effect she or he has on others | One thing she or he does |

(Inspired by J. Ruth Gendler's *A Book of Qualities*)

Picture Proof

Description of a picture of an important moment	This picture makes me realize that...	Truism

Plunging Into a Different World

What I was doing	What caused the magic transport	Where I found myself	What happened next	What I think now, looking back

Point-by-Point Text Analysis

What I notice about the title	What I notice about word choices	What I notice about the speaker's attitudes	What I notice that changes	What I think it all means

Politely Asking for Change

I notice you do this well	I wish you'd also do this	Evidence that the change is needed	Problems I know you'll face	Why it's still worth it

Problem Awareness

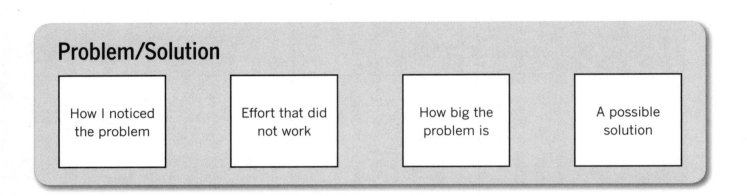

| Problem | Causes | Effects | Possible solutions |

Problem/Solution

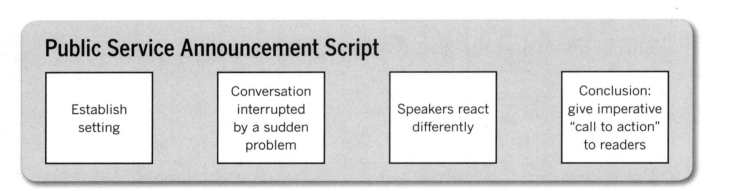

| How I noticed the problem | Effort that did not work | How big the problem is | A possible solution |

Public Service Announcement Script

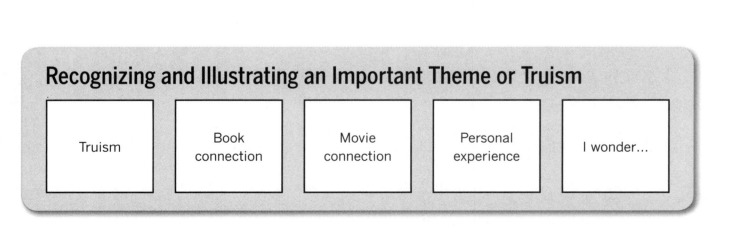

| Establish setting | Conversation interrupted by a sudden problem | Speakers react differently | Conclusion: give imperative "call to action" to readers |

Recognizing and Illustrating an Important Theme or Truism

| Truism | Book connection | Movie connection | Personal experience | I wonder... |

The Story of My Thinking

What I used to think	But this happened	So now I think

Taking a Stand Against Something

Opinion because of A, B, C	How I know A	How I know B	How I know C	Restate opinion

Traditional 5-Paragraph Essay

Opinion because of A, B, C	How I know A	How I know B	How I know C	Restate opinion

Traditional 5-Paragraph Essay Minus One

Opinion because of A and B	How I know A	How I know B	Opinion intensified, renamed

Two Sides of a Coin

| Scenario illustrating a problem | Another way to look at the problem | Scenario illustrating the new way to look at the problem | Advice |

Using a Question and Answer to Frame an Argument

| Opinion | Reasons for opinion | New question | Answer to the question | Restate opinion |

Venting a Problem/Finding a Solution

| My frustration about something | One detail about how bad it is | What I don't understand about it | My plan for solving it |

What's So Special About This Activity

| My opinion about the activity | One thing about the activity | Another thing about the activity | My opinion (once more, with feeling) |

Why I Admire Someone

| Whom I admire | Internal characteristics of that person | External skills he or she has | The effect this person has on me |

Why This Is My Favorite Activity

| I like to _____ | My first experience with it | How you do/play it | How it makes you feel | Positive results |

Why This Season Is My Favorite

| Opinion because of A, B, C | How I know A | How I know B | How I know C | Restate opinion |

Writing a Descriptive Lead

| A person I'm close to | Three physical descriptions | Two inner character traits |

Appendix C: Lessons by Writing Trait and Level of Difficulty

NARRATIVE					
Craft Lesson	Author	Student Essay Topic	Trait	Difficulty Level	Page
1. Color It Up	Elizabeth Stewart	Fishing With Grandpa	O	BASIC	14
2. Sprinkling Writing With Humor	Aine Britton	Rex	V	BASIC	16
3. Adding Movement and Sound to Animate a Piece	Alyssa Lewis	Monkey Pajamas	WC	BASIC	18
4. Using Asides	Anjelica Saj King	Baby Bird Funeral	SF	INT	20
5. Combining Rhetorical Devices: Cataloguing and Repetition	Ashlea Cooper	Cruel Camping	SF	INT	22
6. Using Literary Characters to Write Fiction	Cherilyn Song	Helping Dorothy	ID	ADV	24
7. Using Specific Language From a Special Setting	David Bobo	Treesong	WC	INT	26
8. Using Varied Sentences Openers to Create Rhythm and Flow	Efrata Mola	Injured Foal	SF	BASIC	28
9. Using Precise Language to Create Visual Snapshots	Elizabeth Cummins	Climbing Cliffs	ID	BASIC	30
10. Using Foreshadowing to Create Mood	Jarod Rakoff	Finding Snowball	V	INT	32
11. Building Suspense in a Narrative Through Questions and Answers	Kassidy Acosta	Christmas Swim	O	INT	34
12. Using Participles and Participial Phrases	Lydia Moss	Maui	SF	ADV	36
13. Using Variety When Introducing Narrator Thoughts	Madeleine Mehaffey	Soccer/Inner Strength	SF	INT	38
14. Using Metaphor to Illuminate a Life Lesson	Maria Sierra	Uncle's Funeral	WC	ADV	40
15. Writing Observations	Rachel Denman	Skeleton Bone	O	INT	42
16. Adding Rich Dialogue to a Narrative	Sarah Kelel	New Friend	O	BASIC	44
17. Writing From the Point of View of a Fictional Character	Ashley Davis	Nursing Home	V	INT	46
18. Using Variations of "Said"	Elizabeth Lankford	Abby	WC	BASIC	48
19. Using Depth and Detail to "Explode" a Moment	Cady Fuller	I Do	O	BASIC	50
20. Showing How a Character Changes	Cecelia Balencia	Basketball Camp	V	ADV	52
21. Using Introspection in a Memoir	Cristina Turbeville	Water Dangers	ID	ADV	54
22. Using Onomatopoeia as an Organizational Device	Flor Celeste Saucedo	Bang, Pow, Zoom	O	BASIC	56
23. Using a Story to Illustrate a Life Lesson	Jenna	Spooky Camp Story	ID	INT	58
24. Combining Action and Back-Story	Judith Ann Horton	Lost Cave	O	ADV	60

Craft Lesson	Author	Student Essay Topic	Trait	Difficulty Level	Page
25. Showing Conflicting Feelings in a Personal Narrative	Madeline Smith	Mimi	ID	INT	62
26. Fleshing Out a Kernel Essay With Dialogue	Magen Gross	Ten Worms	O	INT	64
27. Showing How a Character Makes an Important Decision	Mason Corliss	Mousetrap	ID	ADV	66
28. Choosing Vivid Verbs	Raymond Barringer	Present for Mom	WC	BASIC	68
29. Writing Dialogue With Inner Reactions	Sarah Jara	Spelling Bee	O	BASIC	70
30. Using Time Transitions: Flash Forward	Soo (Serena) Chae	Spicy Seafood	O	INT	72
31. Using Absolutes as Sentence Fragments	Stefan Compton	Dirt Bikes	WC	ADV	74
32. Using Time Transitions: Flashbacks	Taylor Agan	Rock Star	O	INT	76
33. Withholding and Revealing Information to Build Suspense	Tyler Clark	History's Ship	O	INT	78
34. Using Anadiplosis to Make a Truism Chain	Zachary Lara	All Stars	SF	ADV	80
35. Using Enumeratio to Add Detail	Keri Petersen	Tae Kwon Do	SF	BASIC	82
36. Layering Thinking and Dialogue	Cassie K. Liesman	Lindsey	O	INT	84
37. Using Transitions to Develop a Conclusion	Elisa Leal	Timothy Toad	SF	ADV	86
38. Weaving Together Text From Different Genres	Sherilynn Moore	Lord's Prayer	O	ADV	88

INFORMATIVE/EXPLANATORY

Craft Lesson	Author	Student Essay Topic	Trait	Difficulty Level	Page
39. Sharing Culture Through Special Events	Arik Rosenberg	Purim	O	BASIC	92
40. Explaining a Historical Context	Angelica Fuentes	Magna Carta	O	BASIC	94
41. Using Compound Predicates in a Series	Hannah Dowding	Towering Hearts of Animals	SF	INT	96
42. Analyzing Characters by Writing Letters Between Them	Hannah Dowding and Karsyn Queen	*Matilda* Letters	O	ADV	98
43. Tracking a Changing Thought Process	Isabella Pedregon	Death of Meatball	ID	BASIC	100
44. Responding to Literature: Questioning the Author (Part I)	Maggie Davis	*I Am the Ice Worm*	O	ADV	102
45. Responding to Literature: Questioning the Author (Part II)	Josh Behn	*The Last Olympian*	V	ADV	104
46. Conversing With an Imagined Listener	Karishma Patel	Theatre Class	ID	INT	106

Craft Lesson	Author	Student Essay Topic	Trait	Difficulty Level	Page
47. Explaining a Concept From the Point of View of a Character	Aaron Eddings	Katniss on Hunger	ID	ADV	108
48. Writing About Clues That Reveal a Situation	Caleb Boles	Divorce	ID	ADV	110
49. Writing a Letter Using Second-Person Point of View	Sarah Cavanaugh	Dear Dalia	WC	BASIC	122
50. Using Personification to Turn an Abstract Concept Into a Colorful Character	Shanice Hubbard, Kaleb Benish, and Tre Staples	Fear, Inspiration, Faith	ID	ADV	114
51. Writing a Graphic Book Review	Batya Katz	*Mission Road*	ID	INT	116
52. Analyzing Literature: Focusing on Character Tension	Eileen Stolow	*The Help*	ID	INT	118
53. Responding to Literature: Characters Conversing About a Problem	Gertrude Washington	Gale/Billy Letters	ID	ADV	120
54. Analyzing Literature: Identifying Character Conflicts	Petronila Juarez	*The Glass Castle*	ID	ADV	122
55. Analyzing Literature: Noticing an Author's Choices	Sylvan Gurinsky	*The Amulet of Samarkand*	ID	BASIC	124
56. Recognizing and Illustrating an Important Theme	Ale Braun	People's Perfections	ID	BASIC	126
57. Analyzing the Rhetorical Effects of Poetic Devices	Alison Reimer	"Annabel Lee"	O	ADV	128
58. Analyzing a Movie	Justin Johns	*The Good, the Bad, and the Ugly*	ID	BASIC	130
59. Creating an "All About" Essay	Landri Bishop	Eyes	O	BASIC	132
60. Giving Writing Vocal Qualities	Mary Burk	Singing	V	INT	134
61. Using Opinions and Facts When Explaining Something New	Sidney Bauer	Facebook	ID	ADV	136
62. Defining an Important Concept	Adrian Gonzales	Pallbearer	SF	ADV	138
63. Writing an Epistolary Essay	Justin Gallego	Abraham Lincoln	ID	INT	140
64. Moving Between Concrete Details and Abstract Ideas	Elisa Leal	PB&J	V	ADV	142
65. Using Quotations to Support a Thesis in a Literary Essay	Selena Portillo	*Animal Farm*	ID	ADV	144
66. Writing an Extended Apostrophe	Steve Carson	Dear Death	O	ADV	146
67. Multimedia Analysis of a Literary Theme	Annie Adams	*Of Mice and Men*	ID	ADV	148

OPINION/ARGUMENT

Craft Lesson	Author	Student Essay Topic	Trait	Difficulty Level	Page
68. Using Facts as Evidence	Meredith Yoxall	Homelessness 1	O	INT	154
69. Using Formal Versus Informal Language	Meredith Yoxall	Homelessness 2	V	BASIC	156

Craft Lesson	Author	Student Essay Topic	Trait	Difficulty Level	Page
70. Writing a Script for a Public Service Announcement	Meredith Yoxall	Homelessness 3	C	ADV	158
71. Examining Quotations	Laura Rodriguez	Versions of Quiet	O	BASIC	160
72. Developing Sentence Variety	Daniel Bonilla	Cyclaws	SF	INT	162
73. Using Personal Experiences to Support Opinions	Arianna V. Issitt	Saturdays	ID	BASIC	164
74. Using Verbs and Adjectives to Back Up Opinions	Devyn Moore	Joan of Arc	ID	BASIC	166
75. Making a Claim About a Historical Event	Sofia Quintanilla	King Henry II	ID	INT	168
76. Using Sensory Details	Katie Briley	Autumn	ID	BASIC	170
77. Using Parentheses	Maryssa Tuttle	Sock Monkey	C	INT	172
78. Naming and Renaming	Savannah Murphy	Barbie	WC	BASIC	174
79. Using an Innovative Format	Wyatt Gillingham	Skateboard Interview	O	ADV	176
80. Using Internal Citations	Abbie Farrimond	Homework 1	C	INT	178
81. Drawing Editorial Cartoons	Abbie Farrimond	Homework 2	ID	INT	180
82. Knocking Down the Opposition	Avery Myers	Animal Adoptions	ID	INT	182
83. Using Quirky Mental Images in an Argument	Lee Kaplan	Sleep	WC	INT	184
84. Using a Question and Answer to Frame an Argument	Lorelei Diener	Uniforms	O	ADV	186
85. Writing a Letter to Raise Awareness About a Social Problem	Madison Morris	Animal Shelters	ID	BASIC	188
86. Using Reptition (Anaphora) for Emphasis and Style	Phillip Kaplan	Library Books	SF	BASIC	190
87. Keeping an Argument From Sliding Into a Personal Narrative	Tori Shiver	Interrupting	ID	BASIC	192
88. Creating a Poster for Persuasion	Will Rymer	Hunting for Food	ID	BASIC	194
89. Using Analogies to Show, Not Tell	Felicia Valdez	Understanding Parents	ID	ADV	196
90. Anticipating and Overcoming Objections	Hagan Cousin	Allowance	ID	INT	198
91. Anticipating a Reader's Objections	Stetson Click	Guitar	ID	INT	200
92. Using Hyperbole for Effect	Jeret Wright	Nolan Ryan	WC	BASIC	202
93. Discovering a Problem, Proposing a Solution	Jordan Powell	Trash	ID	INT	204
94. Weaving Information Into a Persuasive Argument	Katie Weishaar	School Uniform Letter	ID	ADV	206

Craft Lesson	Author	Student Essay Topic	Trait	Difficulty Level	Page
95. Writing a Descriptive Lead	Kazmine Godwin, Kagen Burkett, and Melody Johns	Leads	ID	BASIC	208
96. Using Third-Person Examples in an Argument	Nicholas Reimer	Phones	O	BASIC	210
97. Using Opposites (Antithesis) to Make an Impact	Toni Zimmerman	Alcoholism	SF	ADV	212
98. Revising an Argument for Length	Tyler Moore	Pacific Trash	O	ADV	214
99. Using the Literary Present Tense to Present an Argument	Brittany Duke	*Mockingjay*	WC	ADV	216
100. Making Inferences From Pictures	Barrett Hardy	Photo	ID	BASIC	218
101. Supporting an Argument With Expert Knowledge	Ben McSween	Hunting Hogs	ID	INT	220

Key:

6 Traits	Difficulty Level
ID: Idea Development	BASIC: Basic
O: Organization	INT: Intermediate
SF: Sentence Fluency	ADV: Advanced
WC: Word Choice	
V: Voice	
C: Conventions	